Nelson Cole

Kabbalah
The Mystical Journey of the Soul to Infinity

Original Title:
Cabala- O Mapa Espiritual do Universo
Copyright © 2025, published by Luiz Antonio dos Santos ME.

This book is a non-fiction work that explores the mystical tradition of Kabbalah, offering a comprehensive study of its principles, the structure of the universe, and the path to spiritual transformation. Through in-depth analysis, the author provides insights into key Kabbalistic concepts, including the Tree of Life, the Four Worlds, and the role of divine names in shaping reality.

1st Edition
Production Team
Author: Nelson Cole
Editor: Luiz Santos
Cover Design: Studios Booklas / Ethan Green
Consultant: Jonathan Weiss
Researchers: Sarah Cohen, Daniel Myers, Leah Friedman
Typesetting: Michael Carter
Translation: Rachel Thompson
Publication and Identification
Kabbalah - The Spiritual - The Mystical Journey of the Soul to Infinity
Booklas, 2025
Categories: Kabbalah / Jewish Mysticism
DDC: 296.16 - **CDU:** 296.835
All rights reserved to:
Luiz Antonio dos Santos ME / Booklas
No part of this book may be reproduced, stored in a retrieval system, or transmitted by any means—electronic, mechanical, photocopying, recording, or otherwise—without prior written permission from the copyright holder.

Summary

Systematic Index 4
Prologue 10
Chapter 1 Introduction to Kabbalah... 13
Chapter 2 The Tree of Life and the Ten Sefirot.......................... 22
Chapter 3 Duality and Unity in the Kabbalistic System 32
Chapter 4 The Four Worlds of Kabbalah..................................... 42
Chapter 5 The Role of Divine Names in Kabbalah 52
Chapter 6 Angels and Demons in the Kabbalah 62
Chapter 7 The Soul in Kabbalah Nefesh, Ruach, Neshamá....... 73
Chapter 8 Tikun Olam The Kabbalistic Mission of Correction. 84
Chapter 9 Reincarnation in Kabbalah 95
Chapter 10 The Secret Language of Kabbalah Gematria 106
Chapter 11 Evil and Free Will in Kabbalah............................... 117
Chapter 12 Cabalistic Healing and the Sefirot........................... 127
Chapter 13 Kabbalah and Psychology The Integration of the Ego
.... 138
Chapter 14 The Path of the Righteous Tzadik in Kabbalah..... 150
Chapter 15 The Hidden Wisdom of the Psalms........................ 161
Chapter 16 Kabbalah and the Cycle of Jewish Holidays 174
Chapter 17 The Power of Hebrew Letters 184
Chapter 18 Kabbalah and Dreams 196
Chapter 19 The Path of Repentance Teshuvah in Kabbalah.... 208
Chapter 20 Kabbalah and the Role of Women 220
Chapter 21 The Zohar The Book of Splendor........................... 231

Chapter 23 The 72 Names of God 253
Chapter 24 Kabbalah and the Future 264
Chapter 25 Final Reflections The Kabbalistic Journey 275
Epilogue 285

Systematic Index

Chapter 1: Introduction to Kabbalah - Introduces the vast system of Kabbalah, a mystical tradition of Judaism that seeks to unravel the secrets of the universe and the human soul, and its profound transformative potential.

Chapter 2: The Tree of Life and the Ten Sefirot - Explores the Tree of Life, a central symbol of Kabbalah that represents the mystical structure of the universe and the human soul, and the ten Sefirot, divine emanations that channel energy through the spiritual and physical realms.

Chapter 3: Duality and Unity in the Kabbalistic System - Discusses the concept of duality in Kabbalah, where opposing forces coexist and interact continuously, and the ultimate goal of achieving unity through the integration of these opposing forces.

Chapter 4: The Four Worlds of Kabbalah - Introduces the Four Worlds of Kabbalah - Assiyah (Action), Yetzirah (Formation), Beri'ah (Creation), and Atzilut (Emanation) - which represent different stages of manifestation of spirit in the physical world and different levels of spiritual reality.

Chapter 5: The Role of Divine Names in Kabbalah - Explores the Divine Names in Kabbalah, which are not just titles or forms of identification, but vehicles of divine energy that carry the power to shape reality and influence spiritual forces.

Chapter 6: Angels and Demons in the Kabbalah - Discusses the role of angels and demons in Kabbalah, spiritual beings that act as intermediaries between the higher worlds and the physical world, influencing human life and the functioning of the cosmos.

Chapter 7: The Soul in Kabbalah Nefesh, Ruach, Neshamá - Delves into the Kabbalistic view of the human soul, which is seen as a multifaceted manifestation of spiritual energies, composed of several levels or layers, each representing a different aspect of the human being's spiritual existence.

Chapter 8: Tikun Olam The Kabbalistic Mission of Correction - Explains the concept of Tikkun Olam, the "repair of the world," which is one of the central pillars of Kabbalistic practice, reflecting the belief that creation is an ongoing process, and that human beings have an active role in restoring the harmony and perfection lost in creation.

Chapter 9: Reincarnation in Kabbalah - Explores the concept of reincarnation, or Gilgul, in Kabbalah, which is seen as part of the ongoing process of spiritual correction and evolution of the soul, where the soul goes through various incarnations to complete its spiritual missions and correct the flaws accumulated in previous lives.

Chapter 10: The Secret Language of Kabbalah Gematria - Introduces Gematria, a system of Kabbalistic numerology that assigns numerical values to Hebrew letters, allowing the scholar to find spiritual correspondences between seemingly unrelated words, phrases, and concepts.

Chapter 11: Evil and Free Will in Kabbalah - Discusses the concept of evil in Kabbalah, which is not simply something to be destroyed or eradicated, but rather a necessary function in the cosmos, a force that, when understood and mastered, becomes a catalyst for spiritual growth and the manifestation of free will.

Chapter 12: Cabalistic Healing and the Sefirot - Explores the concept of healing in Kabbalah, which is seen as a profound and multidimensional process, involving not only the physical body but also the spirit and soul, intrinsically linked to the Tree of Life and its ten Sefirot.

Chapter 13: Kabbalah and Psychology The Integration of the Ego - Discusses the integration of the ego, a central theme in Kabbalah and modern psychology, where the ego is not simply a negative force to be eradicated, but rather a vital aspect of the human soul that needs to be understood and integrated in a balanced way.

Chapter 14: The Path of the Righteous Tzadik in Kabbalah - Explores the concept of Tzadik, or "the righteous one," in Kabbalah, a spiritual figure who has achieved a high level of righteousness and acts as a channel between the divine and the material world, positively influencing the cosmic balance.

Chapter 15: The Hidden Wisdom of the Psalms - Discusses the role of Psalms in Kabbalah, which are seen as portals to access deep spiritual dimensions and connect with the divine forces that shape the universe.

Chapter 16: Kabbalah and the Cycle of Jewish Holidays - Explores the Jewish holidays in Kabbalah, which are not just religious celebrations, but powerful spiritual portals associated with specific energies that offer the practitioner the opportunity to achieve spiritual elevation, purification, and transformation.

Chapter 17: The Power of Hebrew Letters - Delves into the power of the Hebrew alphabet in Kabbalah, where each letter is more than a linguistic symbol; it is a creative force, with specific spiritual energy and the ability to influence the physical and spiritual worlds.

Chapter 18: Kabbalah and Dreams - Discusses the role of dreams in Kabbalah, which are considered direct messages from the unconscious and the spiritual world, communication channels between the soul and the higher dimensions.

Chapter 19: The Path of Repentance Teshuvah in Kabbalah - Explores the concept of Teshuvah, or repentance, in Kabbalah, a profound process of spiritual return to the state of unity with the Divinity, repairing spiritual flaws and realigning with the soul's higher purpose.

Chapter 20: Kabbalah and the Role of Women - Discusses the role of women in Kabbalah, which is seen in a profound and central way, with a particular emphasis on the connection with divine feminine energies, recognizing and revering the creative and spiritual force inherent in women.

Chapter 21: The Zohar The Book of Splendor - Introduces the Zohar, the Book of Splendor, one of the central works of Kabbalah and Jewish mysticism, which presents a profound vision of the mysteries of creation, the human soul, and the interactions between the spiritual and material worlds.

Chapter 22: Kabbalah and Material Prosperity - Explores the relationship between spirituality and material prosperity in Kabbalah, where material prosperity is not only permitted but also encouraged, as long as it is aligned with elevated spiritual values.

Chapter 23: The 72 Names of God - Introduces the 72 Names of God in Kabbalah, a sacred sequence of letters, each containing powerful spiritual energies that can be accessed for transformation, protection, and elevation.

Chapter 24: Kabbalah and the Future - Discusses the Kabbalistic perspective on the future of humanity and global spiritual evolution, where the future is not seen as something fixed and predestined, but as a field of possibilities influenced by individual and collective actions.

Chapter 25: Final Reflections The Kabbalistic Journey - Concludes the book with reflections on the Kabbalistic journey, emphasizing that Kabbalah is not just an esoteric theory but a living practice, a system of self-knowledge and spiritual elevation that encompasses all aspects of existence.

Prologue

Imagine yourself, for a moment, at the edge of a great precipice, facing a vast mystery. You feel the gentle breeze, but there's something deeper in the air, something invisible, pulsating, as if the whole universe is about to whisper secrets to you. This book is the door to that enigma, to a wisdom that transcends time, a truth that cannot be uttered in ordinary words, but that echoes in the hearts of those who seek to understand what lies beyond matter.

The knowledge you are about to unravel is not a mere lesson in spirituality; it is a map to your own being, to the mysteries that lie dormant in the center of your soul and in the farthest recesses of the cosmos. Imagine being able to walk this ancient path, explored by a few, where each step brings you closer to a greater understanding of life and existence.

The Kabbalah, the ancient tradition that you are about to discover, is not a simple esoteric concept. It is the hidden code that permeates all things, from the creation of the universe to the most intimate mysteries of your own soul. It is not just an intellectual study; it is a journey of transformation. Every word you read here has the power to awaken something dormant within you, something that resonates with the essence of existence.

Allow yourself to imagine that everything you know, everything you have already experienced, is only the surface. Below this surface, there is a structure, an invisible pattern, an interconnection of divine forces that moves the universe and your own life. This book will give you the keys to see beyond the visible, to touch what is intangible, and, more importantly, to transform yourself.

This text is not just a reading; it is an initiation. With each page, you will be invited to open new doors within yourself. Prepare to immerse yourself in concepts that will challenge your certainties, that will lead you to rethink your own worldview. The Tree of Life, the spiritual worlds, the angels, the divine names - all these concepts will be revealed to you as pieces of a great cosmic puzzle that, when assembled, reveals a surprising and transforming vision of reality.

And, as you enter this path, remember that the Kabbalah is more than just theory. It is practice, it is life, it is a way of seeing and feeling the world around you. It will teach you that every act, every thought, every intention carries with it a depth that extends beyond what the eyes can see. You will be led to understand that the universe is a web of meanings, and that your role in this great cosmic stage is much more important than you ever imagined.

At this moment, you hold in your hands the power to transform your perception. But the choice to continue is yours. If you decide to go ahead, prepare to have your convictions challenged, to be transported to dimensions of thought that reveal the dormant potential within you.

This book is a portal to a new understanding of reality, where darkness is not the absence of light, but the invitation to discover the hidden brilliance in the shadows.

Allow yourself, then, to be guided. Let the words envelop you and lead you on this sacred journey. The wisdom of the Kabbalah awaits you - ready to reveal ancient mysteries and awaken in you an ardent desire for more, to discover, to feel, to be. This is your moment to cross the threshold and begin a new phase of your existence. Surprising revelations are yet to come. Awaken, and see what lies beyond what you have always believed to know.

Chapter 1
Introduction to Kabbalah

Kabbalah, a mystical tradition of Judaism, is a vast system that seeks to unravel the secrets of the universe and the human soul. Its name derives from the Hebrew word *kabbalah*, which means "reception," alluding to the idea that its teachings are not invented, but received. Kabbalah is understood as wisdom transmitted through generations, offering a path to understanding the divine forces that permeate creation. More than just an academic or theoretical study, Kabbalah is a spiritual practice that aims to profoundly transform an individual's perception of life and reality.

The origin of Kabbalah dates back to ancient Jewish mystics who believed that God revealed himself to the world in layers of knowledge. Each layer needs to be unveiled through spiritual effort and meditation. Among the most important texts that form the basis of Kabbalistic thought are the Zohar, the "Book of Splendor," and the Sefer Yetzirah, the "Book of Creation." These writings are considered central pieces of mystical literature, revealing an esoteric view of the Bible and the creation of the universe.

The Zohar, in particular, is a monumental work that discusses the invisible forces operating in the world and the interaction between God and humanity. Written in Aramaic, the Zohar presents a mystical commentary on the Torah (the first five books of the Bible) and covers issues such as the nature of God, creation, the soul, good and evil, as well as deep spiritual rituals and practices. It has become the cornerstone for those seeking a deeper understanding of the teachings of Kabbalah.

Another fundamental text, the Sefer Yetzirah, addresses the creation of the universe from a linguistic and numerical perspective. It describes how God would have used the 22 letters of the Hebrew alphabet to create the cosmos and the ten Sefirot, which are the divine emanations that make up the structure of the world. This numerical and linguistic system is central to Kabbalah, and the idea that the Hebrew alphabet has creative power goes beyond simple human communication. Each letter carries a spiritual essence, a force capable of shaping reality.

Kabbalah offers a spiritual map, a diagram of creation that can guide human beings on their journey of self-discovery and approach to God. This map is best known as the Tree of Life, a diagram that represents the interaction of the ten Sefirot mentioned in the Sefer Yetzirah. The Sefirot are described as emanations of the divinity that reflect different aspects of God and the universe. Each of these emanations has a specific role in the construction of the cosmos and in the relationship between the Creator and his creations. In Kabbalistic practice, the study and meditation on the Sefirot help to understand the path of return to unity with the divine, since each of them reflects a dimension of existence and the human soul.

Kabbalah is not only a way of studying the divine world, but also a way to understand one's own soul. The concept of "soul" in Kabbalah is complex and multidimensional, being composed of different levels. The understanding of the soul allows the Kabbalist to explore his relationship with God and the world. Kabbalah, therefore, serves as a bridge between the divine and the human, revealing that the microcosm (the individual soul) is a representation of the macrocosm (the divine universe). By delving into the mysteries of Kabbalah, the individual is led to recognize his true essence and to align himself with the divine will.

For Kabbalists, the creation of the universe was an act of divine love, in which God contracted, withdrawing part of His own light to make room for the world. This process is known as *tzimtzum*, a divine contraction that allowed creation. The divine light that remained was then fragmented into various emanations and manifestations that gave rise to everything that exists. Kabbalah teaches that the purpose of human beings is to discover this hidden light within creation and within themselves, restoring the original harmony that was broken during the creation process.

Another central concept of Kabbalah is that of Ein Sof, the infinite God. Ein Sof represents the unattainable aspect of God, beyond any human comprehension. God, in Kabbalah, is seen as both transcendent and immanent, which means that, at the same time that He is beyond our comprehension, He also permeates all creation. The study of Kabbalah is, in essence, the quest to understand this paradox: how can the divine be in everything and, at the same time, beyond everything?

Kabbalah offers a dynamic view of the universe. It is not a static system of rules, but a continuous process of creation and recreation. The role of humanity in this process is vital. According to Kabbalistic teachings, each human being has a mission in the world, a function in the repair of the universe, known as Tikkun Olam, or "correction of the world." The objective is to elevate creation, helping to restore the lost unity between the divine and the mundane. By performing acts of kindness, studying, and meditating on the teachings of Kabbalah, the individual participates in this great mission.

Thus, Kabbalah is not an isolated mystical system. It is part of a religious and spiritual tradition that is deeply connected with everyday practice. Although it is often considered esoteric, its principles have practical implications that affect the way the Kabbalist sees and interacts with the world. The search for self-knowledge, the development of the soul, and active participation in the correction of the world are central to the life of the Kabbalist.

In this way, Kabbalah presents itself as a journey of transformation. It challenges the individual to look beyond appearances, seeking the divine in the depths of the world and of himself. Through the study of its sacred texts and the practice of its meditations, the Kabbalist can begin to unravel the mysteries of creation and find the way back to unity with the divine, following the spiritual map that Kabbalah offers as a safe guide for this inner and universal journey.

The depth of the teachings of Kabbalah goes beyond a simple intellectual understanding; it is a living wisdom that permeates all aspects of daily life. By understanding its principles, the Kabbalist not only connects with mystical truths, but also transforms his own existence. Kabbalistic knowledge is an invitation to action: every thought, word, and deed reflects the divine flow and can be a vehicle for spiritual elevation.

Over the centuries, various schools of thought have emerged within Kabbalah, each with its nuances and interpretations of the sacred teachings. These different approaches expand the possibilities of applying Kabbalah in practical life. Two of the main branches are theoretical Kabbalah and practical Kabbalah. The first, also known as Kabbalat Iyyunit, focuses on understanding metaphysical systems, such as the Tree of Life, the Sefirot, and the Divine Names. The second, called Kabbalat Ma'asit, includes techniques that use the knowledge of the Divine Names, meditations, and amulets to influence the spiritual and material world.

Each of these approaches meets different needs and levels of spiritual development. Theoretical Kabbalah, by dissecting the complexity of creation and divine emanations, invites the practitioner to develop a deep awareness of spiritual forces. Practical Kabbalah, on the other hand, offers concrete tools to align human will with divine will. Although rabbinic tradition generally discourages the use of practical Kabbalah techniques by people who have not yet reached a high level of spiritual purity, the combination of study and practice — when carried out with respect and responsibility — can bring balance between theoretical understanding and spiritual experience.

One of the fundamental pillars of Kabbalah is the idea that everything in the universe is interconnected. Kabbalists teach that the microcosm (the human being) is a reflection of the macrocosm (the universe). This means that each action of the individual reverberates throughout creation, influencing the balance of cosmic forces. This concept is exemplified in the structure of the Sefirot, the divine emanations that permeate all levels of existence, both in the spiritual world and in the physical world. Each Sefirah reflects an aspect of God, creation, and the human soul, and the balance between these emanations is fundamental for harmony in the universe.

Understanding the functioning of the Sefirot and their impact on daily life is one of the first steps in a Kabbalist's spiritual quest. These divine emanations are not isolated entities, but rather part of an interconnected system that reflects the underlying unity of all things. The human being is seen as a co-creator in this system. By performing positive actions, in accordance with Kabbalistic principles, the individual contributes to the harmonization of the Sefirot and the restoration of harmony in the world. On the other hand, negative actions can cause an imbalance in the emanations, generating chaos and distancing the individual from the divine light.

Besides the Sefirot, another key concept in Kabbalah is the idea that each person has a divine spark within them, which is always connected to the infinite source of God, the Ein Sof. However, this connection can be obscured by the challenges of material life and selfish desires. The spiritual goal of Kabbalah is to help the practitioner clear these obstructions and reconnect with their true divine essence. For this, the Kabbalistic spiritual practice proposes meditation and contemplation of the Sefirot, in addition to other rituals that allow the individual to elevate their consciousness and tune in to the divine will.

One of the ways in which Kabbalah proposes this reconnection is through the study of the Zohar. The Zohar teaches that creation was not a single event, but rather a continuous process of divine revelation. The world we know is just an external manifestation of a much deeper and more complex reality, which is accessed through mystical contemplation and spiritual practice. By studying the Zohar, the Kabbalist begins to unravel these hidden levels of reality and to understand how creation is sustained by divine light at all times.

Within everyday life, Kabbalah applies in various ways, often in a subtle manner. One of the most accessible and transformative practices is the concept of *kavanah*, which refers to the conscious intention with which a person performs their actions. According to Kabbalistic teachings, it is not only what is done that matters, but also the motive behind the action. By bringing spiritual intention to mundane activities, the individual elevates even the smallest actions to the category of divine service. For example, by reciting a blessing with full awareness of its meaning and its connection to the divine, the Kabbalist transforms the simple act of eating into a sacred ritual that repairs and elevates creation.

Another vital aspect of Kabbalah in daily life is the search for balance. The Sefirot represent different divine qualities — such as mercy, justice, beauty, and wisdom — and the Kabbalist must learn to manifest these qualities in a balanced way in his life. The practice of Kabbalah teaches that each person has the responsibility to align their actions with the energies of these Sefirot, seeking a state of internal and external harmony. For example, if a person acts with too much severity (associated with the Sefirah of Gevurah), this can unbalance their life and cause suffering for both themselves and others. The Kabbalistic path is the path of balance, where mercy and justice are used in the right measure, generating a harmonious life.

There are also notable differences between the Kabbalistic currents that emerged throughout history, especially between the Kabbalah of Safed, represented by figures such as Rabbi Isaac Luria (known as the Ari), and the older, medieval Kabbalah. Lurianic Kabbalah, for example, introduced concepts such as *tzimtzum* (the divine contraction that allowed creation), the "breaking of the vessels" (the process of fragmentation of the Sefirot), and the idea of Tikkun Olam, the collective effort to repair the fragmented world. These concepts gave Kabbalah a new practical dimension, focused on the active role of human beings in the restoration of cosmic order.

These divergent Kabbalistic currents also reflect different emphases on how the sacred texts should be applied in practical life. While some Kabbalists focus on the esoteric study of scriptures and meditative contemplation, others are more interested in practical applications, such as the use of the Divine Names for protection or healing. Each current offers a unique lens through which the practitioner can explore Kabbalistic wisdom, allowing the study of Kabbalah to be both an intellectual journey and a deeply spiritual experience.

Therefore, Kabbalah, despite its esoteric character, connects directly with everyday life, providing the practitioner with a way to integrate its teachings with practical life. Whether through study, meditation, or acts of kindness and justice, the Kabbalist constantly seeks to elevate their existence, revealing the divine light hidden within each aspect of creation. At each step on this journey, he approaches his deepest essence, aligning himself with the continuous flow of light that emanates from the Ein Sof, the divine infinite.

By embracing Kabbalistic practice, the individual not only transforms himself, but also actively participates in the repair of the world, restoring the lost unity between the divine and the mundane. The journey of Kabbalah is, thus, a path of self-discovery and transcendence, where esoteric knowledge intertwines with everyday life, resulting in a complete and transformative spiritual experience.

Chapter 2
The Tree of Life and the Ten Sefirot

The Tree of Life, or Etz Chaim in Hebrew, is one of the most central and powerful symbols of Kabbalah. It represents the mystical structure of the universe and the human soul, a spiritual map that reveals the divine emanations and the way creation was organized. The Tree of Life is composed of ten Sephirot, which are described as channels through which divine energy flows and manifests in both the spiritual and physical worlds. Each Sephirah is an expression of a divine quality, reflecting a specific aspect of God and the cosmos.

The Tree of Life is visually represented as a diagram composed of ten spheres (the Sephirot) connected by 22 paths, each representing one of the letters of the Hebrew alphabet. These connections show the interdependence and interaction between the Sephirot, which are not isolated but function as an integrated system of forces. Understanding this structure is essential for any practitioner of Kabbalah, as it serves as a key to understanding the functioning of the universe and the role of human beings within it.

The Sephirot are organized into three columns: the right, the left, and the center. The right column is generally associated with mercy and the expansive flow of energy, while the left column represents severity and control. The central column, in turn, reflects the balance between these two opposing forces, maintaining harmony between judgment and compassion. This division shows that the creation of the universe, according to Kabbalah, is not chaotic but organized according to principles of balance and justice.

The first Sephirah at the top of the Tree of Life is Keter, which means "crown." Keter represents the highest point of all creation, the threshold between the Ein Sof (the infinite) and the manifest world. It is the Sephirah closest to the divine light and is associated with the pure will of God, a desire to create and share the light. Keter is beyond direct human comprehension, as it is linked to the unattainable divine, representing the most hidden aspect of God.

Just below Keter are the two Sephirot that form the first pair of opposing forces in the Tree: Chochmah and Binah. Chochmah, which means "wisdom," is on the right and symbolizes the active and creative principle. It is the spark of inspiration, the original thought that arises suddenly, an idea that has not yet been fully developed. Binah, which means "understanding," is on the left and represents the receptive and formative principle. If Chochmah is the flash of inspiration, Binah is the process that organizes and gives shape to that idea, structuring it into a comprehensible concept.

These two Sephirot, Chochmah and Binah, work together, and their balance is fundamental. Chochmah without Binah would be uncontrolled creativity, without structure, while Binah without Chochmah would result in rigidity and stagnation, without room for innovation. This interdependence reflects the need for balance between opposing forces at all levels of existence, from the human mind to the creation of the universe.

Below Chochmah and Binah we find Da'at, a hidden Sephirah, which is not counted among the traditional ten but plays an important role in the balance of the Tree of Life. Da'at means "knowledge" and is the point of integration between Chochmah and Binah. It represents the consciousness that arises when wisdom and understanding come together, creating a complete and deep perception of reality.

Following down the central column, below Keter, is Tiferet, the Sephirah of "beauty" or "harmony." Tiferet is the heart of the Tree of Life and symbolizes the integration between mercy and severity, between the expansive love of Chesed and the restrictive judgment of Gevurah, the Sephirot that are above Tiferet in the right and left columns, respectively. Tiferet is also associated with emotional balance and compassion, representing the love that is tempered by justice and the justice that is softened by love.

Chesed, the Sephirah of mercy and kindness, is located on the right column of the Tree of Life. It is expansive and unlimited, representing the divine benevolence that flows without restrictions. Chesed is the force that drives creation and unconditional love. However, this expansion needs to be balanced by the force of Gevurah, which means "strength" or "judgment." Located on the left column, Gevurah represents discipline, containment, and the limits necessary so that creation does not disintegrate into chaos. The interaction between these two forces—the mercy of Chesed and the severity of Gevurah—is essential for the harmony of the universe.

The perfect balance of these two opposing forces is found in Tiferet, which is often described as the Sephirah associated with the concept of beauty precisely because of its ability to harmonize and balance extremes. Tiferet is also linked to the figure of the Messiah in the Kabbalistic tradition, being the point of mediation between the divine and the human, between heaven and earth. The beauty of Tiferet is the expression of the perfect harmony between the forces of love and justice.

Below Tiferet, we find two Sephirot that represent the more concrete manifestation of spiritual forces: Netzach and Hod. Netzach, which means "eternity" or "victory," is located on the right column and is associated with persistence, movement, and the energy that drives creation forward. It reflects the divine force that ensures continuity and victory over challenges. Hod, which means "glory," is on the left column and represents receptivity, humility, and the ability to reflect the divine light. Netzach and Hod work together as the forces of impulse and reception, which maintains balance in human actions and divine creation.

The last two Sephirot are Yesod and Malchut. Yesod, which means "foundation," is the Sephirah that collects and channels the energies of the higher Sephirot to the physical world. It is the intermediary between the spiritual world and the material world, functioning as a bridge that allows divine forces to be manifested in concrete reality. Yesod is also associated with communication, bonding, and sacred sexuality, representing the creative union between the divine and the human.

Malchut, which means "kingdom," is the lowest Sephirah of the Tree of Life and is linked to the physical and material world. It is through Malchut that all the energies of the higher Sephirot are finally manifested in the world. It represents pure receptivity, the space in which divine forces can fully express themselves. Although Malchut is the last Sephirah, it is not less important; on the contrary, it is fundamental, because it is in the material realm that the divine will is completed.

The Tree of Life, with its ten Sephirot, is more than a simple diagram. It is a symbolic representation of the creative dynamics of the universe and a reflection of the spiritual path that each individual must travel. By understanding and meditating on the Sephirot, the Kabbalist seeks to align his soul with these cosmic forces, bringing harmony and balance to both his personal life and the world around him. Each Sephirah is a gateway to a deeper level of spiritual understanding and an invitation to personal transformation.

Now that the structure of the Tree of Life and the ten Sephirot have been introduced, it is essential to deepen the understanding of each one in more detail. In addition to being abstract concepts, the Sephirot represent energies that can be integrated into the practical life of the Kabbalist. Each Sephirah not only reflects a divine quality but is also a reflection of the characteristics and potentialities that exist in the human being. Meditation and work with the Sephirot allow the practitioner to harmonize these energies in their life, creating balance between the spiritual and the material.

Keter is the principle of creation, and its essence is the pure will of God. It represents the moment before manifestation, the divine impulse that initiates the creative process. For the human being, Keter reflects the highest potential of the soul, the state of pure intention. The practice related to Keter involves the contemplation of the highest will and purpose. When a person aligns their own will with the divine desire, they become a channel for the expression of this creative light. Meditation on Keter can help develop greater clarity of purpose and connection to infinite potential.

Chochmah, wisdom, is the source of all ideas and inspirations. It is a constant flow of intuition and insight that manifests immediately and completely. Chochmah is not something that can be studied or learned directly, but it is an energy that can be awakened. In practical life, Chochmah is the ability to receive instant insights and act from intuitive wisdom. Meditation on Chochmah involves opening to receive the divine light without blockages, allowing intuition to manifest spontaneously. This state of openness can be cultivated through trust and surrender to the flow of divine wisdom.

Binah, understanding, complements Chochmah. If Chochmah is the spark of inspiration, Binah is the process of developing, organizing, and structuring that inspiration into something concrete and understandable. In practice, Binah is related to the ability to analyze, plan, and find solutions to life's challenges. Meditating on Binah helps to deepen the understanding of situations, allowing a clear and detailed view of what is in front of us. By integrating Chochmah and Binah, the Kabbalist balances intuition with logical reasoning, creating a harmonious flow of thought and action.

Da'at, knowledge, despite being a "hidden" Sephirah, plays a crucial role in the integration of these forces. In practical life, Da'at represents consciousness, the ability to perceive and understand phenomena with clarity. It is the point where wisdom and understanding come together, creating a state of true comprehension. To work with Da'at, the Kabbalist seeks to develop a deep awareness of himself and the world around him, maintaining the connection with the divine in all actions. This requires being present and aware in the moment, with a clear perception of the unity that permeates all things.

Chesed, kindness or mercy, is the expansive and generous energy of the universe. At the human level, Chesed represents unconditional love, compassion, and the willingness to give without expecting anything in return. Practicing Chesed involves the act of being generous, both materially and emotionally. Meditation on Chesed helps to develop an open and loving heart, stimulating the flow of kindness in all interactions. However, without balance, Chesed can turn into indulgence or lack of control, so it is essential to harmonize it with Gevurah.

Gevurah, strength or judgment, is the energy that imposes limits and discipline. While Chesed expands, Gevurah restricts, creating structures and molds that are essential for growth and stability. In practical life, Gevurah manifests as the ability to say "no," to establish healthy boundaries, and to exercise self-control. Meditation on Gevurah allows the Kabbalist to learn to be firm and disciplined, without falling into excesses of severity or rigidity. The balance between Chesed and Gevurah is fundamental for a harmonious life, where compassion is guided by wisdom and discernment.

The balance between these two opposing forces is found in Tiferet, which is described as the Sephirah of beauty and harmony. Tiferet represents the point of perfect balance between kindness and judgment, creating a state of balanced compassion. In practice, Tiferet is the ability to see beauty in all things, maintaining harmony between internal and external forces. Meditation on Tiferet helps to develop balanced compassion, which is neither indulgent nor severe, but based on truth and love. This balance is what creates a beautiful and spiritually aligned life.

Netzach, victory or eternity, is the Sephirah of perseverance and willpower. Netzach drives the person to continue their path, even in the face of obstacles. In practical life, Netzach manifests as determination and the ability to overcome challenges, maintaining focus on long-term goals. Meditation on Netzach strengthens persistence and the power to keep moving forward, especially when situations seem difficult or without apparent solution.

Hod, glory, is linked to humility and gratitude. If Netzach is the force that propels us forward, Hod is the ability to step back, reflect, and recognize the value of things and people around us. In practice, Hod represents the acceptance of vulnerability and the humility to recognize that divine power is behind all achievements. Meditation on Hod teaches the importance of gratitude and acceptance, allowing the person to see the beauty and value in the small things and in moments of pause and reflection.

Yesod, the foundation, acts as a bridge between the higher Sephirot and the physical world, manifesting all spiritual energies in the material reality. Yesod is associated with connection, communication, and sacred sexuality, and it is the Sephirah that allows divine creativity to be expressed in the world. In practice, Yesod is the ability to concretize ideas and desires in a balanced and healthy way. Meditation on Yesod strengthens the connection with the higher energies, ensuring that spiritual intentions are manifested in life in an ethical and conscious way.

Finally, Malchut, the kingdom, is the Sephirah that governs the physical and material world. Although it is the last of the Sephirot, Malchut is not a passive Sephirah. It represents pure receptivity, but also the ability to govern and manifest divine energies in the material world. Malchut is the force that gives concrete form to divine purpose and human will. In practical life, Malchut is the ability to be grounded in reality, to live fully in the physical world without losing the connection with the divine. Meditation on Malchut teaches the importance of being present in the here and now, integrating all spiritual lessons into everyday life.

The balance between all these Sephirot is essential. The Kabbalist, by meditating and working with each one of them, not only seeks to understand the different facets of creation but also to integrate these energies into their own life. The Sephirot are not merely metaphysical concepts; they are living forces that are in constant interaction in the universe and within each human being. The role of the practitioner is to learn to recognize these energies and work with them in a conscious, balanced, and harmonious way.

By applying the lessons of the Tree of Life, the Kabbalist not only transforms their inner life but also contributes to the correction of the external world, actively participating in the continuous creation of the universe. The balance between the forces of the Sephirot allows the individual to achieve a state of inner unity, aligning with the spiritual laws that govern reality. In this way, the practice of Kabbalah offers not only an intellectual understanding of creation but a living experience of connection and harmony with the divine, the world, and one's own soul.

Chapter 3
Duality and Unity in the Kabbalistic System

Kabbalah is profoundly marked by the presence of duality, reflecting a worldview in which opposing forces coexist and interact continuously. Light and darkness, good and evil, masculine and feminine—these polarities are essential both in the creation of the universe and in the spiritual development of the individual. However, duality in Kabbalah does not imply an irreconcilable division. On the contrary, it is seen as part of a dynamic process that ultimately aims to achieve unity. This tension between opposites is not something to be feared or avoided, but understood and integrated as a fundamental creative force.

The concept of duality manifests itself in many aspects of Kabbalah, one of the most important being the relationship between the right and left columns on the Tree of Life. As we saw earlier, the right column, which includes the Sephirot Chesed (mercy) and Netzach (victory), is associated with expansion, generosity, and the constant flow of energy. On the other hand, the left column, composed of Gevurah (judgment) and Hod (glory), represents contraction, discipline, and limits. These two columns are opposing forces that, although different, are equally necessary for the creation and maintenance of order in the universe. Neither can exist without the other, and the balance between them is what sustains harmony.

The duality between expansion and contraction, or between mercy and judgment, is reflected on many levels of existence. On the cosmic level, it can be seen in the very creation of the world. According to Kabbalah, God initiated the creative process through *tzimtzum*, the retraction or contraction of His infinite light to make room for existence. This act of contraction was followed by the expansion of creation, where the divine light was channeled through the Sephirot, manifesting in the physical universe. Thus, creation is, by nature, a process of tension between expansive and contractive forces, which need to be in balance for the cosmos to remain stable.

On the human level, duality is equally present. Every individual carries within themselves these opposing forces and constantly lives between the desire for expansion—to express their creativity, kindness, and generosity—and the need to restrict themselves, discipline themselves, and impose limits. Kabbalistic spiritual practice teaches that the goal is not to suppress one of these forces, but to integrate them in a balanced way. True wisdom lies in knowing when to be expansive and when to retreat, when to act with mercy and when to exercise judgment.

Duality also appears in the interaction between the masculine and the feminine. In Kabbalah, these are not just biological characteristics, but archetypal forces present in all aspects of creation. The masculine is associated with active, creative, and giving energy, while the feminine is linked to receptive, nurturing, and formative energy. These energies are not exclusively linked to men or women, but are part of the nature of all human beings and the entire cosmos. On the Tree of Life, the Sephirot belonging to the right column are seen as more masculine, while those on the left column are more feminine. The balance between these forces is fundamental to cosmic and personal harmony.

The relationship between the masculine and the feminine in Kabbalah goes beyond the simple opposition of genders. The Zohar, for example, speaks of the union between Zer Anpin (a masculine aspect of God) and Malkhut (the feminine aspect), which symbolizes the union between the divine and the physical world, between the spiritual and the material. This union is seen as essential for the continuity of creation and for the process of spiritual repair. In Kabbalistic practice, this harmony between the masculine and the feminine is also something that the practitioner seeks to reflect in their inner life, cultivating both the active and receptive forces within themselves.

Another important aspect of Kabbalistic duality is the struggle between light and darkness, good and evil. According to the teachings of Kabbalah, evil is not an isolated external force, but a consequence of imbalance. When the creative forces of the universe become misaligned or when human beings act in a disharmonious way, evil manifests. Evil, in Kabbalah, is not absolute; it exists as a possibility that results from human free will and the fragmentation of divine energies. This view emphasizes human responsibility in restoring balance and transforming negative forces into positive ones.

The process of spiritual elevation and correction of evil is known as *Tikkun*. Through Tikkun, the Kabbalist seeks to identify the areas of their life where there is imbalance and work to correct them, whether through acts of kindness, prayer, study, or meditation. Kabbalah teaches that evil should not be rejected or destroyed, but transformed. This reflects the central idea that duality—even between light and darkness—is, at its core, part of a greater whole. The Kabbalist's work is to recognize the hidden light within the darkness and bring that light to the surface.

Unity, which is the ultimate goal of the Kabbalistic system, can only be achieved after the integration of dualities. Kabbalah teaches that God is absolutely one, but this unity manifests itself through the multiplicity of creation. The Sephirot, although they appear to be separate and opposing forces, are in fact different aspects of a single divine source. Likewise, duality in the material world is an illusion; the ultimate truth is that all opposing forces are, in fact, unified in their essence. This vision of unity is reflected in spiritual practice, where the ultimate goal is to transcend dualistic perception and achieve a consciousness of unity with the divine.

On the personal level, this means that the practitioner of Kabbalah seeks to harmonize the opposing forces within themselves. The balance between expansion and contraction, the masculine and the feminine, light and darkness, creates a state of spiritual alignment in which the soul can unite with the divine light. This process is continuous and requires constant attention to the energies at play, both internally and externally. The Kabbalist recognizes that life is a battlefield between opposing forces, but that this conflict is what generates growth and transformation.

The unity sought in Kabbalah is not an annulment of differences, but a harmonious integration of them. The Kabbalist understands that polarities are necessary for spiritual development and that true fulfillment comes when these forces are brought into harmony. This applies both to individual practice and to the world in general, where the balance between opposing energies results in peace and wholeness.

Therefore, duality, far from being an obstacle, is seen as an essential tool for creation and growth. The practice of Kabbalah teaches how to navigate this terrain of creative tensions, using wisdom to balance opposing forces and thus approach divine unity. By learning to work with polarities, the Kabbalist not only elevates themselves spiritually, but also contributes to the balance and harmony of the universe. The journey from duality to unity is, ultimately, the path of return to the divine source, where all distinctions dissolve in the light of the infinite.

Duality, although essential to creation, should not be seen as a definitive state in spiritual life. The goal of the Kabbalist is to learn to integrate these opposing forces, not only in intellectual understanding, but in daily practice, with the aim of achieving inner unity. However, this integration is a process that demands attention and self-knowledge, as it involves recognizing the forces of expansion and contraction, light and darkness, masculine and feminine, within oneself and in the world around.

In daily life, the opposing forces of creation manifest in internal conflicts, external challenges, and emotional tensions. One of the first steps in working with these forces is to recognize that duality is not something to be eliminated, but an opportunity for growth. The human being, like the universe, is made up of these polarities, and balance is only achieved when there is a conscious acceptance of these forces. Kabbalah teaches that these tensions are a vital part of the process of spiritual elevation and that attempting to escape them can result in stagnation.

One of the most effective Kabbalistic methods for dealing with these internal forces is meditation on the Sephirot of the Tree of Life. As previously discussed, the Sephirot represent different aspects of creation and the human soul. Each of them carries a particular energy, and the goal is to achieve a dynamic balance between these energies. For example, if a person realizes that their life is excessively focused on boundless generosity (a manifestation of Chesed), this can lead to exhaustion or lack of discernment. Balance is found by cultivating the force of Gevurah, which brings discipline and healthy boundaries.

This work of internal balancing is not simply a mental or abstract process, but must be reflected in daily actions and decisions. The duality between expansion and contraction can be experienced in common situations, such as how to deal with relationships, work, and personal responsibilities. The Kabbalist who is aware of these energies at play will be able to make more balanced decisions, without falling into the extremes of indulgence or rigidity. This balance, however, is not a fixed formula, but something that must be adjusted continuously, depending on the circumstances and the spiritual needs of each moment.

Kabbalah offers several teachings on how to integrate these opposing forces into a conscious spiritual practice. One of the central concepts in this process is *kavanah*, or intention. By bringing a clear intention to each action, the practitioner transforms even the simplest acts into opportunities for spiritual elevation. When one acts with kavanah, the duality between the sacred and the profane dissolves, and all actions, however mundane they may seem, become channels of expression for the divine forces. This state of unified consciousness allows the practitioner to bring harmony to their life, integrating mercy and judgment, action and receptivity.

Another crucial aspect of this process is the recognition of inner shadows, or the "negative forces" that reside in the human psyche. In Kabbalah, negative forces are not seen as something to be simply repressed or destroyed, but as opportunities for transformation. Evil, or darkness, is the result of imbalances and fragmentations in the soul, and spiritual work involves identifying these areas of shadow and working with them constructively. The transformation of evil into good is one of the pillars of Tikkun, the spiritual correction that aims to restore harmony in the universe.

Kabbalistic meditation practices, such as contemplation of the Sephirot or invocation of the Divine Names, are powerful tools for recognizing and integrating these shadows. For example, by meditating on Tiferet, the Kabbalist seeks to achieve a state of balanced compassion, where justice and mercy are not in conflict, but in harmony. Similarly, by working with Netzach and Hod, the practitioner learns to balance determination and persistence with humility and gratitude. These spiritual exercises help to bring light to areas of internal darkness, promoting a process of healing and elevation.

Furthermore, Kabbalah emphasizes the importance of balancing masculine and feminine energies within oneself. Regardless of gender, every individual carries these two archetypal energies. The masculine, represented by the active, expansive, and creative force, must be balanced by the feminine, which symbolizes receptivity, intuition, and the ability to nurture. When these aspects are unbalanced, there may be internal conflicts, dissatisfaction, and lack of spiritual direction. The Kabbalist who integrates the masculine and the feminine within achieves an inner unity, allowing these energies to flow freely and manifest in a healthy way.

This balance between the masculine and the feminine is also fundamental in interpersonal relationships. Kabbalah teaches that relationships are mirrors of the opposing forces that inhabit each individual. The tension that arises in human interactions is often a reflection of the imbalance between these internal energies. Therefore, relationships, especially the most intimate ones, are seen as an opportunity for spiritual growth, where the individual can learn to balance their own polarities by dealing with the other. Harmony in relationships, according to Kabbalah, can only be achieved when there is an integration of the opposing energies within each person.

In addition to meditative practices and kavanah, Kabbalah offers other tools for dealing with duality and working towards unity. One of them is the practice of Kabbalistic prayer, where the practitioner uses Divine Names and specific formulas to align their will with the divine will. These prayers are seen as a means of harmonizing the forces of the universe, bringing light to areas of darkness and creating a state of spiritual equilibrium. By invoking these Divine Names with a pure intention, the Kabbalist can access energies that help to dissipate darkness and restore unity.

The concept of *Tikkun Olam*, or the correction of the world, also applies to the process of integrating duality. As the individual works to balance their own internal forces, they contribute to the restoration of balance in the external world. Kabbalah teaches that the microcosm (the human being) reflects the macrocosm (the universe), and each act of personal correction has a direct impact on the harmony of the universe. Thus, the spiritual work of the Kabbalist is not only an individual path, but a collective responsibility. Personal transformation leads to the transformation of the world, and inner unity reflects cosmic unity.

Finally, the quest for unity in Kabbalah is a continuous journey of integration. It is not about achieving a static state of perfection, but about learning to navigate the opposing forces of life with wisdom and balance. Duality is an intrinsic part of creation, and the Kabbalist, by accepting and working with these polarities, moves towards an ever deeper state of unity. The ultimate goal is to transcend the limited perception of separation and duality, achieving a consciousness that all forces, whether of light or darkness, masculine or feminine, are expressions of a single divine source.

This state of unity, known as *achdut*, is the pinnacle of the Kabbalistic spiritual path. It is the perception that all divisions are illusory and that, behind all polarities, there is a unifying truth. By achieving this consciousness, the Kabbalist not only finds inner peace, but also contributes to the restoration of peace and harmony in the world. Duality, once integrated and balanced, dissolves in the infinite light of the Ein Sof, revealing the essential truth that all is one.

Chapter 4
The Four Worlds of Kabbalah

Kabbalah offers a profound and multifaceted view of creation, dividing existence into four main levels known as the Four Worlds. These worlds reflect different stages of proximity to the divine and are fundamental to understanding the process of manifestation of spirit in the physical world. Each world represents a distinct spiritual reality and corresponds to a layer of the relationship between the Creator and creation. These Four Worlds are: Assiyah (Action), Yetzirah (Formation), Beri'ah (Creation), and Atzilut (Emanation). Together, they describe the journey of divine energy from its purest state to its concretization in the material plane.

The first world, Assiyah, is the world of action and materiality. It corresponds to the physical and sensory plane, where creation manifests in a tangible form. Assiyah is the realm of actions and consequences, the plane in which human choices are concretized and events occur according to natural and spiritual laws. In the Kabbalistic system, this is the world furthest from the original divine light, being marked by density and duality. However, it is here that the spiritual mission is concretized, as it is in this world that the incarnated soul has the opportunity to perform actions to transform and elevate its own existence and the environment around it.

Yetzirah, the second world, is the world of formation. At this level, creation is not yet physical, but begins to gain shape and definition. Yetzirah is the plane of emotions, invisible forces, and energies that shape reality. This is the domain of angels and spiritual entities that help direct and influence the flow of energy in the universe. Yetzirah is also associated with the plane of human emotions, being the meeting point between the mind and the heart. The influences of Yetzirah shape our feelings and emotional reactions, and it is in this world that the Kabbalist can begin to perceive how their emotions and thoughts affect their physical reality.

The third world, Beri'ah, is the world of creation. Here, divine energy begins to take shape in abstract concepts and ideas, but is not yet shaped in a physical form. Beri'ah is the realm of the mind and understanding, where the ideas and thoughts arise that will eventually manifest in the lower planes. This world is closely related to the Sefirah Binah, understanding. At the human level, Beri'ah is where the deepest concepts of existence, spiritual wisdom, and insight develop. The mind is able to reach new levels of understanding on this plane, but still needs Yetzirah and Assiyah to concretize these thoughts into actions in the physical world.

The fourth and highest of the worlds is Atzilut, the world of emanation. This is the world closest to the divine source, the purest and most abstract plane of existence, where the light of God is not yet veiled.

Atzilut is the domain of the higher Sefirot and uncorrupted divine energy, where everything is still part of the divine unity. At this level, there is no separation between Creator and creation; divine emanations flow directly from the source. Atzilut is associated with the Sefirah Chochmah, pure and intuitive wisdom, and reflects the state of consciousness in which duality does not exist, and everything is perceived as part of the divine whole.

These Four Worlds are not physical places, but levels of consciousness and existence that coexist simultaneously. The human soul, according to Kabbalah, has the ability to move between these worlds, depending on its level of spiritual development and its ability to elevate its consciousness. In its most basic state, the soul resides in the world of Assiyah, operating on the physical and sensory plane. As the soul purifies and elevates itself, it can reach the more subtle levels of Yetzirah, Beri'ah, and finally, Atzilut, where union with the divine is more direct.

Each of the worlds has its own structure and hierarchy, being governed by different forces and spiritual entities. In Assiyah, for example, we find the natural forces and angels that oversee the physical world, while in Yetzirah, the spiritual forces linked to human emotions and feelings are more active. In Beri'ah, abstract creation and ideas are at the center of attention, while Atzilut is purely a state of unity with the divine essence. Thus, the interaction between these worlds directly influences both the macrocosm (the universe) and the microcosm (the human being).

The spiritual journey of the Kabbalist, therefore, is not just a search for intellectual understanding, but a conscious effort to elevate the soul through these levels of existence. The ultimate goal is to reach Atzilut, the world of emanation, where the soul can experience unity with God. To achieve this elevation, Kabbalah offers various practices, including meditation on the Sefirot, prayer with *kavanah* (focused intention), and the deep study of sacred texts. These practices allow the Kabbalist to expand their consciousness and access the higher worlds, bringing more light and clarity to their life on the material plane.

The idea that the Four Worlds are interconnected also implies that our actions in the world of Assiyah can affect the higher levels of Yetzirah, Beri'ah, and Atzilut. Kabbalah teaches that every action, thought, and emotion generates a spiritual impact that reverberates through the worlds. When a person acts in a conscious and spiritual way, they elevate not only themselves, but also the environment around them, contributing to the elevation of the physical world. Likewise, actions devoid of spiritual consciousness can create blockages that prevent the flow of energy between the worlds.

This view of the interconnectedness of the worlds reflects the importance of individual responsibility within the Kabbalistic system. *Tikun Olam*, the concept of correcting the world, is a collective mission, but it begins with individual correction. By elevating their own consciousness and working to balance their emotions and actions, the Kabbalist contributes to the harmonization of the higher worlds and to the repair of the universe. The elevation of the soul through the Four Worlds is not just an individual journey, but a process that benefits all of creation.

The study of the Four Worlds also offers the Kabbalist a detailed map of the spiritual journey. Knowing at which level of consciousness the soul is operating allows the practitioner to identify the obstacles and challenges that need to be overcome in order to advance. By understanding how the worlds are interconnected, the Kabbalist can use this wisdom to adjust their spiritual practice and daily life, so as to align their consciousness with the higher levels of existence.

Thus, the Four Worlds of Kabbalah are not just a theoretical explanation of the universe, but a practical tool for spiritual transformation. They provide a clear path for the elevation of the soul, offering insights into the nature of existence and the relationship between the divine and the material. By meditating on the Four Worlds and seeking to integrate their teachings into daily life, the Kabbalist begins to see reality with new eyes, perceiving the underlying unity of all things and finding their role in the grand scheme of creation.

Now that the Four Worlds of Kabbalah have been presented—Assiyah, Yetzirah, Beri'ah, and Atzilut—it is time to delve deeper into the interconnection between them and understand how the Kabbalist can consciously transit through these levels of existence.

Each of the Four Worlds is associated with a specific level of consciousness. When the soul is in the world of Assiyah, it is immersed in physical action and sensory experiences. It is here that the Kabbalist's choices materialize, where each act has a tangible impact on the environment. However, Assiyah is not a world disconnected from the others. The actions performed on this plane reverberate in the higher worlds, influencing Yetzirah, Beri'ah, and Atzilut. Therefore, the spiritual work of the Kabbalist begins in Assiyah, where their conscious actions and intentions create the foundation for elevation in the higher worlds.

One of the most effective ways to transit between the worlds is through Kabbalistic meditation. Each world represents a layer of reality, and by meditating with clear intention, the Kabbalist can move their consciousness from one level to another. By focusing on a specific world, the practitioner can access its energies and bring its influence to the physical plane. For example, by meditating on the qualities of Yetzirah, the world of emotions and formation, the Kabbalist can harmonize their emotions and learn to better deal with the emotional challenges that arise in Assiyah. This reflects the interconnection between the worlds, where changes made at one level of consciousness affect the other levels.

Meditation on the Sefirot is also an essential tool for navigating the Four Worlds. Each Sefirah reflects a divine quality and is present at all levels of existence, from Atzilut to Assiyah. By meditating on a specific Sefirah, such as Tiferet (beauty and harmony), the Kabbalist accesses its expression in all worlds simultaneously. In the world of Atzilut, Tiferet represents pure and spiritual harmony; in Beri'ah, the idea of beauty and balance begins to form; in Yetzirah, these qualities manifest in balanced emotions; and, finally, in Assiyah, Tiferet manifests as tangible beauty and harmony in the Kabbalist's life.

This process of elevating the soul requires a careful balance. It is not enough for the Kabbalist to simply aspire to the higher levels of existence; it is necessary to integrate the lessons of each world in a practical way. Each time the soul ascends, it also brings something back to the physical world. This reflects the Kabbalistic idea that spirituality should not be disconnected from everyday life. The true Kabbalist is one who can live in Assiyah—the world of action—while remaining conscious of their connection to the higher levels of Yetzirah, Beri'ah, and Atzilut.

A practical example of how this interconnection works can be seen in the concept of *Tikun Olam*, the correction of the world. *Tikun Olam* is both an individual and collective effort to restore harmony in the universe. When a person performs a good deed with the intention of elevating their soul, they not only impact the world of Assiyah, but also influence the higher worlds. The act of giving charity, for example, may seem like a simple physical action, but when performed with *kavanah* (spiritual intention), it awakens a correction in the spiritual levels. The divine energies that flow from Atzilut are directed to the physical world, bringing light and harmony to all levels of existence.

In addition to meditation, prayer is another powerful tool that the Kabbalist uses to transit between the worlds. Kabbalistic prayer is different from a simple supplication; it involves the conscious use of Divine

Names and the recitation of specific passages that reflect the energies of the higher worlds. During prayer, the Kabbalist connects with the energies of Atzilut and channels this light to the lower levels. This process creates a bridge between the divine and the human, allowing the practitioner to act as a channel for spiritual forces, elevating their soul and contributing to the correction of the universe.

Another important aspect of this spiritual journey is the understanding of the spiritual bodies that correspond to the Four Worlds. The human soul, according to Kabbalah, has several levels, each corresponding to one of the worlds. The physical body and the *Nefesh* soul are associated with Assiyah. The emotional body and the *Ruach* soul correspond to Yetzirah, while the intellectual soul, *Neshamah*, is linked to Beri'ah. Finally, the highest soul, *Chayah*, which is the spark of divine unity, is connected to the world of Atzilut. The Kabbalist works to purify and elevate each of these spiritual bodies, allowing their soul to ascend to higher levels of consciousness.

Each of the worlds also has its own spiritual challenges that the Kabbalist must overcome. In Assiyah, the challenge lies in the tendency to get lost in materiality and the distractions of the physical world. In Yetzirah, the Kabbalist must deal with unbalanced emotions and learn to master the emotional plane. Beri'ah presents the challenge of refining thought and avoiding intellectual pride, while in Atzilut, the greatest challenge is the very dissolution of the ego, for at this level the Kabbalist must abandon all sense of separation and unite with the divine will.

Furthermore, the Four Worlds of Kabbalah are not static; they influence and interconnect in a constant flow of energy. The prayers of the Kabbalistic tradition, such as the *Shemoneh Esrei* or the *Kaddish*, reflect this interaction. Each prayer is structured to take the soul on a spiritual journey that traverses the Four Worlds, connecting the practitioner to the forces of Atzilut and bringing that light back to Assiyah. The Kabbalist, by praying with *kavanah*, not only elevates their own soul, but also influences the spiritual correction of the entire universe.

Another aspect of the interconnection between the worlds is seen in meditative practices with Hebrew letters. Each letter of the Hebrew alphabet is considered a channel for divine energies, and by meditating on these letters, the Kabbalist can access different worlds. The combination of letters creates Divine Names that correspond to different aspects of creation. For example, the Tetragrammaton YHVH is associated with the Four Worlds, with each of the letters representing a different level. Meditating on these letters allows the Kabbalist to connect directly with the divine energies at all levels of creation, from Atzilut to Assiyah.

Therefore, the goal of Kabbalistic practice is not simply to "ascend" to the higher worlds and disconnect from physical reality. On the contrary, true spiritual elevation occurs when the Kabbalist learns to integrate the teachings of each world into their daily life, transforming their actions, thoughts, and emotions according to divine principles. This integration allows the Kabbalist to become a true "channel of light," bringing the wisdom of Atzilut, the clarity of Beri'ah, the emotional harmony of Yetzirah, and the conscious action of Assiyah into their existence.

The journey through the Four Worlds is both a spiritual ascent and a return to unity. By navigating these worlds, the Kabbalist discovers that true elevation is not in escaping the physical world, but in transforming the physical into something sacred. By aligning their consciousness with the highest levels of existence, they draw closer to the divine light and, at the same time, bring that light to the world of Assiyah, fulfilling the greater purpose of creation.

Chapter 5
The Role of Divine Names in Kabbalah

Within the vast Kabbalistic system, the Divine Names occupy a central place, representing one of the most powerful keys to understanding and interacting with creation. These names are not just titles or forms of identification; they are vehicles of divine energy, means by which the Creator manifests different aspects of His essence and governs the universe. Kabbalah teaches that the world was created through speech, and the Divine Names are manifestations of these creative words, carrying the power to shape reality and influence spiritual forces.

Among the Divine Names, the most sacred and central is the Tetragrammaton, the four-letter Name, YHVH (יהוה). This Name is considered so sacred that, in religious contexts, it is never pronounced as it is written. Instead, the term "Adonai" is used in its liturgical reading. The Tetragrammaton is understood in Kabbalah as an expression of the four stages of creation and is directly connected to the Four Worlds—Atzilut, Beri'ah, Yetzirah, and Assiyah—reflecting the process by which divine energy manifests from the highest to the most physical of planes.

Each of the letters of the Tetragrammaton has a profound meaning and is associated with different emanations of the divinity. The first letter, Yod (י), represents the initial point of creation, the origin of pure wisdom that has not yet been manifested. It is connected to the world of Atzilut, the highest of the worlds, where the divine light is still undifferentiated and pure. The second letter, He (ה), is the first manifestation of this wisdom, associated with Beri'ah, the world of creation and understanding. The third letter, Vav (ו), symbolizes the extension of this energy, connected to the world of Yetzirah, the world of formation and emotions. The second He (ה) is the concretization of creation in the world of Assiyah, the plane of action and materiality.

In addition to the Tetragrammaton, other Divine Names have specific functions within the Kabbalistic system. For example, Elohim (אלהים) is the Name associated with the Sephirah Gevurah, which represents judgment and restriction. Unlike YHVH, which reflects the mercy and harmony of creation, Elohim is the Name that expresses the natural laws and the force of discipline. The duality between these two Names—YHVH and Elohim—is a representation of the tension between expansive goodness and restrictive severity that, in balance, sustain the harmony of the universe.

Another important Divine Name is El Shaddai (אל שדי), often associated with the Sephirah Yesod and the concept of foundation and protection. Shaddai has been interpreted as "the one who is sufficient," reflecting the aspect of God that provides and sustains the universe. This Name is used in prayers and Kabbalistic practices aimed at protection and prosperity, creating a connection with the divine forces that sustain creation in balance.

The Divine Names in Kabbalah are frequently used in meditative and ritual practices. The Kabbalist who meditates on a Divine Name is seeking to align his own consciousness with the energy that this Name represents. By invoking the Name YHVH, for example, the practitioner is not just reciting a sacred word, but channeling the energy of mercy, harmony, and unity, bringing these qualities into his life and the world around him. Similarly, the invocation of the Name Elohim seeks to bring discipline, justice, and balance.

In addition to meditations, the Divine Names also play a fundamental role in prayers and blessings. In the Kabbalistic tradition, each Name of God has a specific purpose and is recited with clear intention to channel the correct energy. The Name Adonai (ינדא), for example, is frequently used in prayer contexts to reflect divine sovereignty over the physical world, while Ehyeh Asher Ehyeh (היהא רשא היהא), "I am that I am," is associated with the aspect of God that transcends time and space, expressing the eternal and immutable.

The Divine Names are also connected to different aspects of creation and the human soul. In Kabbalistic practice, there is a deep relationship between the Name YHVH and the structure of the soul. Kabbalah teaches that the human soul is composed of five levels: Nefesh, Ruach, Neshamah, Chayah, and Yechidah. Each of these layers of the soul can be seen as a manifestation of a letter of the Tetragrammaton, reflecting the soul's journey from the physical world to unity with the divine. Meditating on the Divine Names allows the Kabbalist to align his soul with these different energies, facilitating the process of spiritual elevation.

In the context of creation, Kabbalah teaches that the Divine Names are the tools with which God created and sustains the universe. In the Sefer Yetzirah, the "Book of Creation," there is a detailed explanation of how the Hebrew letters and the Divine Names were used by God to give form to the world. The Names are like spiritual building blocks, each carrying a specific function in the grand design of creation. The Tetragrammaton, for example, is considered the most fundamental formula, the "four-letter name" that contains the secrets of the creative process.

Another Name that possesses great power in Kabbalah is the Shem HaMeforash, the "Ineffable Name," which is composed of 72 combinations of three letters. Known as the 72 Names of God, this sequence is considered one of the most powerful tools for connecting with divine energies. Each of the 72 Names reflects a specific aspect of the divinity and can be used for a series of spiritual purposes, such as protection, healing, prosperity, and guidance. These Names are often meditated upon or recited in specific combinations to achieve spiritual and material goals, helping the practitioner align with cosmic energies.

The use of Divine Names in Kabbalah is also linked to Tikkun, the process of spiritual correction. Correctly invoking a Divine Name can restore lost balance, both on an individual and collective level. For example, if a person is facing a period of emotional or spiritual turbulence, meditating on the Name Elohim can help restore balance and order, bringing stability to chaos. Similarly, the Name YHVH is often invoked to bring harmony and mercy to situations where there is suffering or conflict.

One of the great lessons of Kabbalah is that the Divine Names are not magic words that guarantee automatic results. Their power is only revealed when invoked with *kavanah*, that is, with pure spiritual intention and proper focus. The Kabbalist must be in tune with the energy that the Name represents and understand it on a deep level. Furthermore, the Divine Names are not used lightly; they are sacred tools that demand respect and reverence. Improper use or use without clear intention can result in imbalances or even negative spiritual consequences.

In practice, the Divine Names are often inscribed on amulets, used in meditations, or recited in special prayers. These amulets, engraved with specific combinations of Names, are used for spiritual protection, healing, and elevation. Kabbalah recognizes that the Names are channels for divine energies and, therefore, are powerful means of connecting with the spiritual realms, attracting blessings and protection to the practitioner's life. However, it is always essential to remember that the real power lies in the intention and spiritual alignment, and not in the words themselves.

In this way, the Divine Names offer the Kabbalist a direct path of connection with the divine and of influence over spiritual forces. They reflect the different facets of God, from the expansive mercy of YHVH to the judgment of Elohim, and allow the practitioner to consciously work with these energies to achieve balance, harmony, and correction.

Kabbalah offers a vast array of spiritual tools that allow the practitioner to access divine energies through the invocation of the Sacred Names. The proper use of these practices provides the Kabbalist not only with a deeper connection to divine forces but also with the ability to channel these energies to heal, protect, and transform his own life and the world around him.

One of the central aspects of using the Divine Names is meditation. In Kabbalah, meditation with the Divine Names is not just a process of mental reflection, but a deep spiritual practice that involves both the body and the soul. Meditating on a Divine Name allows the Kabbalist to align his own consciousness with the specific aspect of God that the Name represents. For example, meditating on the Tetragrammaton, YHVH, is a way to tune into the qualities of mercy, harmony, and creation. The practitioner visualizes the letters of the Name, contemplates its meaning and function, allowing these energies to flow into his mind, emotions, and body.

To begin a Kabbalistic meditation with the Divine Names, the practitioner must enter a state of mental stillness and clear intention (*kavanah*). Intention is essential, because without it, the practice can become a mechanical act devoid of spiritual power. A common technique involves visualizing the letters of the Name floating before the meditator, shining with divine light.

The practitioner can focus on each letter individually, exploring its symbolic meaning and its correspondence with the spiritual spheres.

For example, in meditation on the Tetragrammaton YHVH (יהוה), each of the letters is associated with one of the Four Worlds of Kabbalah: Yod (י) represents Atzilut (Emanation), He (ה) is linked to Beri'ah (Creation), Vav (ו) reflects Yetzirah (Formation), and the second He (ה) connects to Assiyah (Action). While meditating, the Kabbalist can visualize his consciousness moving through these levels of existence, starting in the divine unity of Atzilut and descending to the physical world of Assiyah, where the energy of the Name is manifested in concrete actions.

In addition to visual meditations, the recitation of the Divine Names is another essential practice in Kabbalah. Reciting a Name with the proper intention and reverence allows the practitioner to activate the energies associated with that Name. However, it is not just about repeating sounds, but about connecting each word to the correct spiritual intention. For example, when reciting the Name Elohim during a meditation on justice or the need for balance, the Kabbalist invokes the power of discipline and cosmic order. Elohim is associated with the Sephirah Gevurah, and by reciting this Name, the practitioner seeks to channel this force of containment and balance into his life.

Each Divine Name has a specific purpose, and its use is adapted according to the spiritual needs of the moment. When there is a need for healing or protection, the Names related to mercy and divine sustenance, such as El Shaddai (ידש לא), can be recited or meditated upon. Shaddai is one of the Names of God that is closely linked to protection and stability, and its recitation creates a kind of spiritual shield. The visualization of the writing of this Name in bright light around the body or a physical space can be used to invoke protection against negative influences or destructive forces.

Another example is the use of the Name Adonai (ינדא), which symbolizes God's dominion over the material world. During prayers, especially in moments of thanksgiving or requests for divine intervention, the Name Adonai is frequently used to connect the practitioner to divine sovereignty over the earth and the physical plane. Invoking this Name helps to bring God's blessings into everyday life, recognizing His control over creation and His ability to directly influence the world of Assiyah.

One of the most powerful and complex sets of Divine Names is the 72 Names of God. These Names, composed of three letters each, are derived from three consecutive verses of the Book of Exodus (14:19-21) and are considered direct channels to divine forces. Each of these 72 Names has a specific spiritual function, such as healing, protection, spiritual elevation, conflict resolution, and much more. For example, the Name Vav He Vav (והו) is associated with opening paths and removing spiritual obstacles. Meditating on this Name or reciting it in moments of blockage or difficulty can bring a renewal of energy and clarity.

To use the 72 Names of God effectively, the Kabbalist must first understand the purpose of each

Name. The practice involves both the recitation and visualization of the corresponding letters, allowing the energy of that specific Name to flow into his life. Some Kabbalistic traditions also use these Names in amulets or talismans, written on scrolls or engraved on objects that the practitioner carries with him for protection or spiritual strengthening.

Furthermore, Kabbalah teaches that the Divine Names have a protective function. During moments of spiritual vulnerability, or when the practitioner finds himself under attack from negative forces, invoking the appropriate Name can generate a field of protection around him. This is especially important in advanced Kabbalistic practices, where the Kabbalist may be dealing with powerful energies that require great care and protection. Invoking Names like El Shaddai or meditating on the 72 Names of God associated with protection creates a spiritual barrier that prevents the entry of negative influences.

The practice of invoking the Divine Names is not exclusive to moments of need or crisis; it is also used for continuous spiritual elevation. During daily prayer, the Kabbalist can integrate different Names into his prayers, elevating his soul towards the highest levels of consciousness. Each recitation must be accompanied by intention and focus, as Kabbalah teaches that spiritual effectiveness is directly linked to the quality of *kavanah*. Praying or meditating automatically, without full awareness of the purpose and meaning, can weaken the spiritual impact of the practice.

Finally, an important aspect of the practical use of the Divine Names in Kabbalah is the care and respect with which they must be treated. It is not recommended to use these Names indiscriminately without proper understanding and preparation. The Kabbalist must approach these practices with reverence, knowing that the Names carry the creative energy of God and that their improper use can result in spiritual imbalance. For this reason, in-depth study, the guidance of a spiritual mentor, and the cultivation of a disciplined spiritual life are fundamental for anyone who wishes to work with the Divine Names effectively.

Therefore, the Divine Names in Kabbalah are sacred tools of great spiritual power. When used with clear intention, focused meditation, and reverence, they offer a direct path to accessing divine energies and transforming them into blessings, protection, healing, and spiritual elevation. These Names are not just words, but portals to the deepest and most fundamental forces of creation, allowing the Kabbalist to actively participate in the correction of the world and the harmonization of reality with the divine plan.

Chapter 6
Angels and Demons in the Kabbalah

In Kabbalah, the universe is populated by a vast array of spiritual entities, of which angels and demons are some of the most important. These spiritual beings act as intermediaries between the higher worlds and the physical world, influencing human life and the functioning of the cosmos. The belief in angels and demons is not exclusive to Kabbalah, but the Kabbalistic system offers a unique perspective on the role and function of these entities, revealing their importance in the spiritual balance of the universe and the journey of the soul.

Angels, in the Kabbalistic view, are divine emissaries who serve as channels for God's light and will. They are described as beings created from pure, divine energy, incapable of making mistakes or acting against the divine will. Each angel has a specific function, usually associated with an aspect of creation or a spiritual task. For example, the angel Michael is traditionally associated with mercy and protection, while Gabriel is linked to justice and judgment. These angels are seen as extensions of the Sephirot, the divine emanations, and their functions reflect the qualities of these Sephirot.

In the Kabbalistic system, angels are not autonomous beings, but agents who carry out the divine will. They do not possess free will, like humans, and their mission is always to fulfill divine decrees, whether in the spiritual or physical world. One of the fundamental texts of Kabbalah, the Zohar, describes angels as channels that carry the prayers of human beings to the higher realms, helping to bring about *Tikkun Olam*, the correction of the world. When a person prays with *kavanah* (deep and conscious intention), the angels are responsible for taking that prayer to its final destination in the divine spheres, where it can be answered according to God's will.

Angels also play a crucial role in spiritual protection. Many Kabbalists believe that each person has guardian angels who accompany them throughout their life, protecting them from negative influences and guiding them in times of difficulty. These protective angels are often invoked in Kabbalistic prayers and meditations. A classic example is the protective prayer known as *Birkat HaMalachim* (Blessing of the Angels), in which angels like Michael, Gabriel, Uriel, and Raphael are asked to be around the person, bringing protection, healing, and enlightenment.

In addition to individual angels, there are also angelic hierarchies. Kabbalah teaches that angels are organized into different orders and categories, each with its own specific functions and attributes. These hierarchies reflect the different layers of creation and the way divine light manifests in the various levels of the universe. Angels of higher orders, such as the Seraphim and the Ophanim, are closer to the divine throne and are charged with maintaining harmony in the highest spiritual spheres. Angels of lower orders, such as the Malachim and the Ishim, interact more directly with the physical world and human life.

Angels are also deeply connected to the Divine Names. Each angel is an expression of a Name of God, and its power derives directly from that Name. This means that by invoking a Divine Name, the Kabbalist is also accessing the angel associated with that Name and its specific function. For example, the angel Raphael, who is associated with healing, is directly linked to the Divine Name El Shaddai, the Name that reflects God's sufficiency and protection. Invoking the Name of El Shaddai, therefore, is also a way of calling upon Raphael's assistance for matters of health and healing.

On the other hand, Kabbalah also recognizes the existence of negative forces, often described as demons or Qlipot. While angels serve as channels for divine light, demons are seen as manifestations of imbalance, fragmentation, and darkness. They inhabit the Qlipot, the spiritual "husks" or "shells" that surround the divine light and obscure it. These negative forces arise when there is a break in the harmony of the Sephirot or when divine energies are misused. Unlike angels, who are entirely good, demons are described as chaotic and destructive forces that represent evil and disorder in the cosmos.

Demons in Kabbalah are not independent beings who directly oppose God. Instead, they are the result of unbalanced or misdirected energies. Kabbalah teaches that, in the process of creation, part of the divine light was "broken" and fell into the Qlipot, resulting in a state of fragmentation. These "husks" imprison the light and create negative forces, which Kabbalists must learn to recognize and correct. In this way, demons are seen as reflections of human free will and its capacity to create imbalance when acting selfishly or destructively.

It is important to understand that demons in Kabbalah are not entities with absolute power over human beings. They are forces of imbalance that can be neutralized or redeemed through *Tikkun*, the process of spiritual correction. When a person acts with negative intention or turns away from the divine light, they can inadvertently feed the Qlipot, strengthening these destructive forces. However, by recognizing these imbalances and engaging in corrective spiritual practices, the Kabbalist can restore harmony and dissipate the influence of the Qlipot.

In Kabbalistic practice, there are several ways to neutralize negative forces or demons. One of them is the use of Divine Names and protective prayers. Invoking Names like Elohim or Adonai in moments of spiritual danger can create a protective barrier that prevents the influence of the Qlipot. In addition, meditation on the higher Sephirot, such as Tiferet (harmony) and Yesod (foundation), can help to rebalance internal and external energies, weakening the presence of negative forces.

Another way to deal with these negative forces is through repentance and spiritual rectification. When a person recognizes that they have acted in a selfish or destructive way, they can engage in the process of

Teshuvah (repentance), returning to the divine light and correcting the errors that fed the Qlipot. Kabbalah teaches that by doing *Teshuvah*, the practitioner not only neutralizes evil but also transforms darkness into light, redeeming the energies trapped in the Qlipot and elevating them back to the Sephirot.

In addition to influencing individual life, angels and demons also play a role in maintaining cosmic order. Angels work to maintain the balance of the Sephirot and ensure that the divine light flows harmoniously throughout the universe. They are the guardians of creation, maintaining order and protecting the harmony between the worlds. Demons, although they create chaos and disorder, also serve a broader purpose, as their presence challenges human beings to act justly and in a balanced way. Kabbalah teaches that without the challenge of negative forces, human free will would have no meaning, and spiritual growth would be impossible.

The spiritual work of the Kabbalist, therefore, involves recognizing the presence of these opposing forces and learning to integrate them harmoniously. Angels are allies in the spiritual journey, guiding, protecting, and supporting the practitioner in their quest for unity with the divine. At the same time, demons represent challenges that must be overcome through spiritual awareness, discipline, and self-control. By balancing these influences, the Kabbalist moves towards enlightenment, helping to restore cosmic order and harmony between good and evil.

Therefore, in Kabbalah, angels and demons are not just mythological or symbolic figures, but profound representations of the energies that permeate the universe and human life. They are reflections of the spiritual forces that operate in the world, and understanding these entities is crucial for any practitioner who wishes to walk with wisdom and discernment on the spiritual path.

Now that we understand the natures and functions of angels and demons in the Kabbalistic system, it is important to explore how the Kabbalist can interact with these spiritual forces in daily practice. This segment delves into the techniques for connecting with angels, neutralizing demonic influences, and maintaining the spiritual purity necessary to work with these entities in a balanced way. Kabbalah offers detailed methods for dealing with both divine messengers and negative forces, allowing the practitioner to navigate the spiritual world safely.

Connecting with angels is one of the most fascinating and practical aspects of Kabbalah. As previously described, angels are divine messengers and guardians of spiritual harmony. To connect with them, the Kabbalist must first understand the importance of spiritual purity. Unlike humans, who possess free will and can deviate from the divine will, angels are pure manifestations of God's energy. This means that interaction with them requires a high level of spiritual intention (*kavanah*) and a mind focused on the purpose of elevation.

One of the most common practices in Kabbalah for invoking the presence of angels is prayer. Prayer not only serves to invoke divine aid, but it is also a way to request the intercession of angels. For example, when reciting the *Birkat HaMalachim* (Blessing of the Angels), the Kabbalist specifically asks that angels like Michael, Gabriel, Raphael, and Uriel come close and bring their blessings of protection, healing, enlightenment, and justice. These prayers are powerful because they channel the specific energies associated with each of these angels and bring them into the physical world, promoting connection with the divine.

Meditation on the angelic hierarchies is another effective method for connecting with these spiritual messengers. Each angel is associated with a Sephirah or a specific aspect of creation. By meditating on a Sephirah, such as Tiferet (harmony) or Gevurah (judgment), the Kabbalist tunes into the spiritual qualities of that sphere and, consequently, with the angels who operate within that energy. To do this, the practitioner can visualize the light of the Sephirah and concentrate on its qualities, allowing the presence of the angels corresponding to that Sephirah to manifest. For example, when meditating on Tiferet, the practitioner can connect with the angel Raphael, whose function is to promote healing and harmony.

Visualizations are an additional technique for creating a bridge between the Kabbalist and the angelic world. During meditation, the practitioner can visualize a circle of light around them, with angels positioned in the four cardinal directions. Each angel has a specific color and purpose. Michael, associated with the element of fire and the south direction, is visualized in a bright red tone. Gabriel, related to water and the north, is seen in deep blue tones. Uriel, angel of earth and the east, appears in gold or brown, while Raphael, the angel of healing and the west, is seen enveloped in an emerald green light. This practice creates a shield of protection around the Kabbalist, allowing them to feel surrounded by angelic presence and protection during moments of spiritual vulnerability.

It is important that, when connecting with angels, the Kabbalist always maintains an attitude of humility and respect. In Kabbalah, angels are not beings to be worshiped, but recognized as extensions of the divine will. They are partners in the spiritual journey, and the Kabbalist should approach them with reverence, knowing that the true source of power is always God. Prayer and meditation help to establish this cooperative relationship, where the angel serves as a guide and protector, but never as an object of veneration.

On the other hand, Kabbalah also teaches effective ways to neutralize demonic forces and undo the influence of the Qlipot. As mentioned earlier, the Qlipot are spiritual "husks" that trap the divine light and cause imbalances. When the Kabbalist recognizes that they are being influenced by negative energies, they must take immediate steps to restore balance.

One of the most effective techniques for dispelling negative influences is the invocation of the Divine Names. The Name Elohim, associated with the Sephirah Gevurah, is often used in moments of tension or when there is a negative spiritual presence. This Name brings an energy of judgment and containment, helping to restore order where there is chaos. By invoking Elohim, the Kabbalist can ward off darkness and the disordered forces that have infiltrated their life. In addition, reciting Psalm 91, known as a prayer of protection against negative forces, is widely used in Kabbalistic traditions to ward off demons and other harmful influences.

Spiritual cleansing is also a fundamental aspect of protection against negative energies. There are Kabbalistic purification rituals that help to remove these unwanted influences. An example of this is the use of the *mikveh*, a ritual bath of purification. Although the *mikveh* is traditionally used in contexts of physical and spiritual purity, it can also be used to cleanse a person of negative energies accumulated over time. Immersing oneself in the *mikveh* with the correct intention (*kavanah*) allows the Kabbalist to reconnect with the divine light and get rid of the Qlipot that obscure their soul.

Another effective method for dealing with demonic forces is the use of Kabbalistic amulets. These amulets, written or engraved with Divine Names or combinations of sacred Hebrew letters, function as protective shields. One of the most common amulets is the one that carries the Name Shaddai (ידש), which is widely used for protection and spiritual security. Carrying or hanging an amulet engraved with the Name Shaddai helps to ward off negative forces and create a field of protective energy around the practitioner.

However, the Kabbalist must always remember that the true effectiveness of the amulet depends on their own intention and spiritual connection.

To strengthen spiritual protection and neutralize demons, exorcism prayers can also be used. In Kabbalah, these prayers are specific invocations that ask for the help of the Divine Names and angels to expel negative energies. Reciting these prayers with *kavanah* is crucial, as they channel the energy of the higher spheres and direct it against destructive influences. In addition, the Kabbalist can meditate on the Sephirot of balance, such as Tiferet and Yesod, to restore internal harmony and thus weaken the influence of the Qlipot.

Another vital aspect of interacting with angels and demons is maintaining a moral and ethical life. Kabbalah teaches that human behavior directly affects the balance between spiritual forces. When a person acts in an altruistic and compassionate manner, they feed the angels that guide their actions. On the other hand, selfish or destructive actions strengthen the Qlipot, creating opportunities for demons to exert their influence. Therefore, Kabbalistic practice emphasizes that the moral life is not just a religious duty, but a spiritual protection against negative forces.

Teshuvah (repentance) is one of the most powerful ways to free the soul from the influence of the Qlipot. When a person recognizes their mistakes and actively seeks to correct their ways, they open space for the divine light to return to their life. The act of repentance, accompanied by prayers and meditations, purifies the soul and dissolves the negative energies that were holding it back. In Kabbalah, repentance not only removes the spiritual consequences of bad actions, but also transforms evil into good, redeeming the fragmented energies and restoring harmony.

Interaction with angels and demons in Kabbalah is an essential part of the spiritual path, requiring discernment, purity of intention, and a deep commitment to spiritual practice. Angels are powerful allies who guide and protect the Kabbalist on their journey, while demons represent challenges and obstacles that must be overcome through discipline and rectification. Understanding and applying these practices allows the Kabbalist not only to grow spiritually, but also to contribute to the correction of the world, dissipating darkness and bringing divine light to creation.

Chapter 7
The Soul in Kabbalah
Nefesh, Ruach, Neshamá

Kabbalah offers a profound and complex vision of the human soul, which is seen as a multifaceted manifestation of spiritual energies. Unlike the common understanding of the soul as a single, indivisible entity, Kabbalah teaches that the soul is composed of several levels or layers, each representing a different aspect of the human being's spiritual existence. These levels are known as Nefesh, Ruach, and Neshamah, and each has its distinct function, its relationship with the physical body, and its connection to the spiritual universe.

The first and most basic level of the soul is the Nefesh, which can be described as the "animal soul." Nefesh is intimately connected to the physical body and the biological functions of the human being. It is the vital force that animates the body, controlling instinctive and physical processes. The Nefesh is responsible for our basic needs, such as eating, sleeping, and self-preservation. This layer of the soul is most connected to the world of Assiyah, the plane of action and materiality, reflecting the most earthly and immediate concerns of human existence. However, even though it is the most "basic" layer, the Nefesh should not be seen as something negative. It is the foundation of life, and without it, the soul could not exist in the physical plane.

Although the Nefesh is responsible for the most instinctive aspects of life, it also contains the potential for spiritual development. The purification of the Nefesh is the first step in the Kabbalist's spiritual journey. The goal is to elevate this level of the soul, refining the instincts and desires so that they do not dominate the person, but rather are integrated harmoniously with the higher levels of the soul. Kabbalistic meditation and self-improvement practices are used to transform the energies of the Nefesh from mere animal instincts into something more spiritualized, allowing the person to become more aware of their connection with higher spiritual dimensions.

The second level of the soul is the Ruach, which can be translated as "spirit" or "wind." The Ruach is the emotional and moral layer of the soul, related to emotions, character, and personality. It is higher than the Nefesh and acts as a bridge between the physical body and the higher spiritual realms. While the Nefesh is linked to physical needs, the Ruach is responsible for our emotions, aspirations, and the ability to discern good and evil. It is related to the plane of Yetzirah, the world of formation, where emotional and psychic forces are at play.

The Ruach is where the human being's emotional qualities are refined and developed. Kabbalistic practice teaches that it is necessary to control and balance emotions so that they do not become destructive forces. Instead of succumbing to anger, envy, or selfishness, the

Kabbalist seeks to cultivate positive emotions such as love, compassion, and gratitude. The Ruach is also associated with the capacity for moral discernment, allowing the human being to make ethical choices and live in accordance with divine principles. Through the elevation of the Ruach, the practitioner learns to overcome negative emotions and to live in a balanced and harmonious way, connecting with higher spiritual energies.

The third and highest level of the soul is the Neshamah, which means "divine soul." The Neshamah is the level closest to God and is connected to higher intelligence and spiritual consciousness. It represents the divine spark that resides within each human being, the part of the soul that is always in contact with the highest spheres of existence. The Neshamah is linked to the world of Beri'ah, the world of creation, where pure ideas and abstract concepts begin to take shape.

The Neshamah is the source of spiritual wisdom and deep understanding of reality. When a person accesses the Neshamah, they rise above earthly concerns and begin to see life from a broader and more spiritual perspective. This level of the soul allows the Kabbalist to perceive the underlying unity of all things, connecting with the divine purpose and experiencing a deep sense of peace and harmony. However, accessing the Neshamah is not a simple task. It requires years of spiritual practice, meditation, and the overcoming of the lower levels of the soul, such as the Nefesh and the Ruach. Only when these levels are purified and balanced can the Kabbalist truly experience the level of the Neshamah.

Each of these three levels of the soul—Nefesh, Ruach, and Neshamah—is interdependent. The Nefesh provides the physical basis necessary for life; the Ruach allows emotions and moral values to guide the person's actions; and the Neshamah connects the soul to the divine and the greater purpose of existence. Although each level has its own characteristics, they are not isolated. The Nefesh, for example, can influence the Ruach, just as the Ruach can influence the Neshamah. Kabbalistic practice seeks to harmonize these three levels, allowing them to work together in a balanced and harmonious way.

The process of spiritual elevation in Kabbalah involves the purification and integration of these three levels of the soul. The Kabbalist must first work on the level of the Nefesh, controlling their desires and instincts so that they do not dominate them. Then, they must cultivate and refine the Ruach, balancing their emotions and developing a strong sense of morality. Finally, they can focus on the Neshamah, seeking spiritual wisdom and direct connection with the divine. This process is continuous and requires discipline, patience, and dedication. However, as the Kabbalist advances on their journey, they get closer and closer to their true spiritual purpose.

Kabbalah teaches that the soul is not just a passive entity that exists within the body; it is active and dynamic, constantly interacting with the spiritual worlds and the universe around it. When a person engages in spiritual practices, they not only elevate their own soul but also contribute to the elevation of the world. This concept is linked to Tikkun Olam, the process of spiritual correction that aims to restore harmony in the universe. By purifying and elevating their soul, the Kabbalist helps to correct the imperfections of the world and to bring more divine light into creation.

In addition to Nefesh, Ruach, and Neshamah, Kabbalah also mentions two other levels of the soul that are higher and less accessible to most people. These levels are Chayah and Yechidah. Chayah is related to the level of spiritual unity, where the person experiences life as a direct expression of divine will. Yechidah, in turn, is the highest level of the soul, where the person experiences absolute unity with God, with no distinction between the individual and the Creator. These levels, however, can only be accessed by individuals who have reached a very advanced state of spiritual development.

Therefore, the Kabbalistic view of the soul is not only a description of our inner nature but a detailed map for the spiritual journey. Understanding and working with the levels of the soul—Nefesh, Ruach, and Neshamah—allows the Kabbalist to navigate the dimensions of existence, rising from earthly desires to divine wisdom. The soul, in Kabbalah, is the link between the human being and the divine, and by nurturing and purifying this connection, the practitioner gets closer and closer to the light of God and the true purpose of their life.

Now that the three levels of the soul – Nefesh, Ruach, and Neshamah – have been introduced, it is necessary to delve deeper into how each of these levels can be elevated and purified, allowing the Kabbalist to connect more deeply and consciously with their spiritual essence. Kabbalah not only describes the structure of the soul but also offers practical tools to refine these levels, guiding the individual on their journey of spiritual growth.

The Nefesh, as the most basic level of the soul, represents the life force and is intimately connected to the physical body and instincts. It is the first point of contact between the soul and the material world. The elevation of the Nefesh does not imply the rejection of physical or instinctive needs, but rather the refinement of these energies so that they can serve a greater spiritual purpose. Kabbalah teaches that, when the Nefesh is in its purest state, it allows the individual to maintain a healthy balance between their physical desires and their spiritual aspiration.

Kabbalistic practice offers several ways to purify the Nefesh. A central method is ethical and moral discipline, known as Mussar. By following the precepts of justice, kindness, and self-improvement, the individual gradually transforms their instinctive tendencies into behaviors aligned with the divine will. Control over impulses, such as anger, envy, or excessive desire, is fundamental to this transformation. Kabbalah suggests that the Nefesh be channeled through constructive actions, such as the practice of charity (Tzedakah) and involvement in acts of kindness (Chesed), which help to purify the soul at its most instinctive level.

In addition to ethical discipline, meditation also plays a crucial role in the purification of the Nefesh. Meditations focused on the body and breath help to bring greater awareness of physical and emotional needs, allowing the practitioner to address them in a balanced and conscious way. By meditating on the Sefirah Malkhut, which is associated with the physical world and the Nefesh, the Kabbalist can focus on harmonizing their physical energies with their spiritual purpose, learning to govern their body and desires with wisdom.

After the Nefesh, the Ruach, the emotional and moral level of the soul, must also be purified. The Ruach is responsible for emotions and the capacity for moral discernment, and its elevation depends on the Kabbalist's ability to refine their emotions and develop an elevated moral character. One of the main challenges of this level is the balance of emotions. Emotional imbalances, such as excessive attachment, anger, or fear, can block the flow of spiritual energy and hinder the development of the Ruach.

The practice of emotional self-assessment is essential for the development of the Ruach. This involves a regular analysis of one's own emotions and motivations, in order to recognize and transform feelings that may be unbalanced. Kabbalah suggests that the Kabbalist contemplate emotions in light of the Sefirot, identifying which Sefirah a particular emotion is based on and how it can be balanced. For example, excessive anger can be seen as an imbalance in the Sefirah Gevurah (strength and restriction), and to balance it, the practitioner should seek to cultivate the qualities of Chesed (mercy and kindness), which soften and harmonize the energy of Gevurah.

In addition to self-assessment, the Ruach can be elevated through the practice of prayer. In Kabbalah, prayer is not just a request, but a form of spiritual elevation that aligns human emotions with the divine will. When we pray with kavanah (focused intention), we are not only expressing our feelings but also refining and purifying our emotions as we connect with higher spiritual energies. Daily prayer, especially those involving the use of the Divine Names, helps to regulate emotions and develop a deeper sense of inner balance and harmony.

Finally, the Neshamah, the highest level of the soul accessible in everyday life, requires a different kind of spiritual work. While the Nefesh deals with physical needs and the Ruach with emotions and character, the Neshamah is related to wisdom and direct connection with the divine. The elevation of the Neshamah requires the Kabbalist to transcend material limitations and attain a higher state of consciousness.

The most important practice for elevating the Neshamah is the contemplation and study of sacred texts, especially the Zohar and the Sefer Yetzirah, which contain the mysteries of creation and the nature of the soul. The study of these texts is not just an intellectual exercise, but a means of accessing deeper levels of consciousness. By engaging with these texts, the Kabbalist expands their mind and soul, approaching the divine wisdom that resides in the Neshamah. Kabbalah teaches that the study and meditation on the divine mysteries awaken the Neshamah, allowing the person to see the world with a spiritual clarity that transcends earthly concerns.

Another practice associated with the Neshamah is deep meditation on the higher Sefirot, such as Chochmah (wisdom) and Binah (understanding). These Sefirot are directly connected to the Neshamah and represent the highest levels of spiritual understanding. Meditating on these Sefirot allows the Kabbalist to tune their soul to the highest frequencies of creation, facilitating a deeper connection with the divine. During these meditations, the practitioner visualizes the divine light descending through the Sefirot and filling their mind and soul with wisdom and clarity.

Furthermore, the Neshamah is elevated through the development of a contemplative life, where the person seeks to continuously align with the divine purpose. The Kabbalist who lives with this awareness not only elevates themselves spiritually but also influences the world around them. Kabbalah teaches that, when the Neshamah is awakened, the person acts as a channel of light, bringing wisdom and harmony to those around them and helping to restore balance in the universe.

It is important to remember that the three levels of the soul – Nefesh, Ruach, and Neshamah – are not separate entities, but are intimately interconnected. The Nefesh, for example, influences the Ruach, and the Ruach, in turn, affects the Neshamah. Therefore, the purification and elevation of the soul require a holistic effort. The Kabbalist must work on all levels simultaneously, integrating physical, emotional, and spiritual needs into a coherent practice.

Furthermore, the process of spiritual elevation is continuous. The soul, according to Kabbalah, is always in motion, ascending and descending through the different levels of existence. Even when a person reaches a high state of consciousness, they still face challenges and opportunities for growth. Kabbalistic spiritual practice teaches that every action, thought, and emotion has the potential to elevate or lower the soul, depending on the intention and awareness behind it.

The purification of the lower levels of the soul is a prerequisite for accessing the higher levels. This means that, although the Kabbalist may aspire to the wisdom of the Neshamah, they must first ensure that their Nefesh is purified and that their Ruach is balanced. Only when these more basic layers are in harmony can the Kabbalist begin to access the deeper mysteries of creation and the soul.

The ultimate purpose of the elevation of the soul in Kabbalah is unification with the divine. Through the work of purification and elevation, the Kabbalist seeks to return to their true essence, the divine spark that resides in the Neshamah. When this unification is achieved, the person experiences a deep integration between the body, mind, and spirit, living in alignment with the divine purpose and contributing to cosmic harmony.

Therefore, the spiritual journey of elevating the Nefesh, Ruach, and Neshamah is a continuous process of refinement and transformation, where the Kabbalist, by aligning their life with divine principles, finds not only inner peace and harmony but also true spiritual fulfillment.

Chapter 8
Tikun Olam
The Kabbalistic Mission of Correction

At the heart of Kabbalah lies the idea of *Tikkun Olam*, which can be translated as "correction of the world" or "repair of the world." This concept is one of the central pillars of Kabbalistic practice, reflecting the belief that creation is an ongoing process, and that human beings have an active role in restoring the harmony and perfection lost in creation. *Tikkun Olam* is not limited to the physical dimension, but also encompasses the spiritual world, uniting the microcosm (the individual) with the macrocosm (the universe). Through personal spiritual elevation and corrective actions in the physical world, the Kabbalist contributes to the correction of the universe as a whole.

To understand *Tikkun Olam*, it is necessary to return to the concept of the breaking of the vessels (*Shevirat HaKelim*), described in Kabbalah as a primordial moment in the process of creation. According to Kabbalistic tradition, before the existence of the universe, everything was contained in the infinite light of God, called *Ein Sof*. However, when God wished to create the world, the divine light was channeled into spiritual "vessels" that were meant to contain and manifest this light. However, the vessels were not able to contain the intensity of this divine energy and, thus, they broke, causing the "breaking of the vessels" and the dispersal of the divine light into fragments. These fragments of light, called *Nitzotzot* (sparks), became trapped in the *Qlipot*, the spiritual "shells" that obscure the light.

Tikkun Olam, then, refers to the process of gathering these sparks of light and freeing them from the *Qlipot*, restoring the lost harmony of creation. This process of correction is a continuous spiritual work, involving both the individual and humanity as a whole. Kabbalah teaches that each person has the responsibility to participate in this *Tikkun*, whether through personal improvement, spiritual elevation, or concrete actions in the physical world that promote justice, kindness, and harmony.

The role of the human being in *Tikkun Olam* is unique because, unlike angels or other spiritual entities, humans possess free will. This means that the individual can choose to act in a constructive or destructive way. Every choice a person makes has the potential to elevate or lower spiritual reality. When someone acts with divine intention (*kavanah*) and with elevated purpose, their actions not only correct their own behavior but also liberate sparks of light trapped in the *Qlipot*, contributing to the overall correction. On the other hand, selfish and destructive actions feed the *Qlipot* and hinder the process of correction.

One of the most powerful ways to participate in *Tikkun Olam* is through the *Mitzvot*, the divine commandments. In Kabbalah, each *Mitzvah*, when performed with spiritual intention, contributes to the release of the sparks of light and to the correction of the world. The *Mitzvot* are not seen merely as ethical rules or religious rituals, but as tools for spiritual elevation. When a person fulfills a *Mitzvah*, be it an act of charity, a prayer, or even the act of maintaining a pure thought, they are participating in the process of restoring harmony in creation.

The concept of *Tikkun Olam* is also intimately linked to free will. Kabbalah teaches that the creation of evil and negative forces, represented by the *Qlipot*, is not a mistake, but an intentional part of the divine plan. These negative forces exist to give human beings the opportunity to exercise free will, choose good, and thus contribute to the correction of the world. The duality between light and darkness, good and evil, is necessary for *Tikkun Olam* to be possible. Without the possibility of choosing evil, good would have no meaning, and the process of correction would have no purpose.

An important aspect of *Tikkun Olam* in Kabbalistic practice is meditation on the *Sefirot* and the Divine Names. Each *Sefirah* represents an emanation of the divine light, and meditating on these emanations is a way to restore the balance between them and bring more light into the world. Kabbalistic practice also involves the use of the 72 Names of God, which are considered powerful spiritual tools for correction. These Names, when invoked with pure intention, help to channel spiritual energies that can correct distortions and release the light trapped in the *Qlipot*.

In addition to spiritual practices, *Tikkun Olam* also manifests in concrete actions in the physical world. Kabbalah teaches that social justice and altruism are essential parts of the process of correction. When a person acts with kindness and promotes justice in their community, they are directly contributing to the elevation of the world. Kabbalah makes no distinction between the spiritual and the material; on the contrary, it teaches that both are interconnected. Actions in the physical world have spiritual repercussions, and *Tikkun Olam* involves both inner transformation and the improvement of the external conditions of society.

Shabbat, the holy day of rest in Judaism, is an example of how *Tikkun Olam* is reflected in daily practice. In Kabbalah, Shabbat is seen as a moment of cosmic correction, where the physical and spiritual worlds align harmoniously. During Shabbat, the divine light flows more freely, and the individual has the opportunity to reconnect with the divine source. By observing Shabbat with the correct intention, the Kabbalist participates in *Tikkun Olam*, restoring the balance between the upper worlds and the physical world.

In addition to individual practices, Kabbalah also sees *Tikkun Olam* as a collective process. The correction of the world cannot be accomplished by a single person; it is a global effort that involves all of humanity. Kabbalah teaches that all of creation is interconnected, and the *Tikkun* of one person positively affects the world around them. Similarly, the corruption of one soul negatively affects the universe. Therefore, the correction of the world depends on both personal and collective effort. When entire communities work to elevate themselves spiritually and act justly, they accelerate the process of *Tikkun Olam*.

Tikkun Olam also has messianic implications in Kabbalah. Kabbalism teaches that the final *Tikkun*, the complete correction of the world, is linked to the coming of the messianic era. This era will be marked by the total liberation of the divine sparks from the *Qlipot* and by the restoration of perfect harmony between the physical and spiritual worlds. Although each generation has the responsibility to work towards *Tikkun*, the messianic era represents the culmination of this process, where evil will be transformed into good and the light of God will shine fully throughout creation.

Finally, *Tikkun Olam* reflects Kabbalah's optimistic view that, despite challenges and difficulties, the world is in a continuous process of returning to perfection. The Kabbalist, by participating in this process, not only transforms their own life but also contributes to the spiritual evolution of all creation. This spiritual work is seen as the highest purpose of the human being, who, by participating in *Tikkun Olam*, becomes a co-creator with God, helping to bring more light and harmony to the world.

The understanding that the physical and spiritual worlds are interconnected, and that every action has a cosmic impact, is at the heart of the concept of *Tikkun Olam*. It is not just a call for personal transformation, but a global mission that involves every human being. By living in accordance with the spiritual principles of

Kabbalah, each individual can play their part in this grand process of correction, bringing the world back to its original state of divine perfection.

Having introduced the concept of *Tikkun Olam* as the Kabbalistic mission of correcting the world, we will now delve into the practical techniques that allow the Kabbalist to actively participate in this process, both on a personal and collective level. Kabbalah offers a series of spiritual and practical tools that help the individual to carry out the necessary correction in their life and, at the same time, contribute to the spiritual elevation of the world. These practices range from specific meditations to ethical and moral actions in daily life.

The first and perhaps most essential Kabbalistic practice for *Tikkun Olam* is the development of spiritual awareness. In Kabbalah, this is called *daat*, or deep knowledge. Developing *daat* means increasing awareness of one's own actions, thoughts, and intentions, so that everything we do is aligned with the purpose of correction. This implies living with *kavanah*, focused intention in every action, be it a prayer, an act of charity, or a daily interaction. When we act with *kavanah*, our actions become vehicles for the release of the divine sparks that are trapped in the *Qlipot*, the "shells" that obscure spiritual light.

One of the most powerful practices of spiritual elevation is prayer with *kavanah*. Prayer in Kabbalah is not seen as a simple recitation of words, but as an active process of connection with the upper worlds. When a person prays with *kavanah*, they direct their spiritual energy to the heavens, aligning their will with that of

God. Prayer becomes a channel for the release of the sparks of light that are trapped in the physical world. A classic example of this is the *Sh'ma* prayer ("*Sh'ma Israel, Adonai Elohenu, Adonai Echad*"), which is central to Judaism and Kabbalah. By reciting the *Sh'ma* with full intention, the Kabbalist reaffirms the unity of God and participates in the *Tikkun*, elevating the soul and contributing to the correction of the universe.

In addition to prayer, meditation on the *Sefirot* is another essential practice. As we have seen, the *Sefirot* are the divine emanations that govern different aspects of creation. Meditating on the *Sefirot* allows the Kabbalist to align with these energies and restore spiritual balance both internally and in the world around them. For example, meditation on *Chesed* (mercy) can be used to soften a situation of severe judgment (associated with *Gevurah*). By meditating on the *Sefirot*, the practitioner helps to maintain the harmonious flow of divine light, releasing the energies that have been blocked by the *Qlipot*.

Another Kabbalistic practice linked to *Tikkun Olam* is the use of the Divine Names in meditations and prayers. Each Name of God reflects a specific divine quality and, by invoking them, the Kabbalist attracts this energy to the physical world. The 72 Names of God are particularly powerful in this process. Each of these Names is a combination of three Hebrew letters that function as channels of spiritual energy. Meditating on one of the 72 Names, visualizing its letters and pronouncing them with the correct intention, can help to solve specific problems, such as healing, protection, or the spiritual elevation of a situation. These Names are direct tools of correction, allowing the Kabbalist to act as an agent of transformation both in their life and in the reality around them.

Tikkun Olam is also carried out through the *Mitzvot*, the divine commandments. In the Kabbalistic view, each *Mitzvah* is a means of restoring spiritual order in the universe. By fulfilling a *Mitzvah* with intention and devotion, the Kabbalist releases a spark of light from the *Qlipot* and directly contributes to the correction of the world. Some *Mitzvot* are especially important in this process, such as *Tzedakah* (charity), which is seen as a way of balancing judgment with mercy. Kabbalah teaches that when a person gives *Tzedakah*, they are not only helping the other, but also elevating themselves and the universe around them. The act of giving, performed with pure intention, dissolves the rigidity of the *Qlipot* and allows the light to flow more freely.

In addition to spiritual practices, *Tikkun Olam* also requires concrete actions in the physical world. Kabbalah does not separate the spiritual from the material; on the contrary, it teaches that both are interconnected and that physical actions can have a direct impact on the spiritual world. This is reflected in the idea that social justice and altruism are fundamental parts of the *Tikkun*. When a person acts justly, treats others with dignity, and promotes harmony in society, they are releasing divine sparks and contributing to the collective elevation of the world.

A practical example of this is the Kabbalistic commitment to Shabbat. Shabbat is seen as a "taste" of the final *Tikkun*, the messianic era, when all of creation will be restored to its original perfection. During Shabbat, physical work ceases, and attention is directed towards rest and spiritual contemplation. Shabbat represents the perfect balance between the physical and spiritual worlds, where the forces of creation align harmoniously. By observing Shabbat, the Kabbalist participates in a cosmic correction, elevating the world to a state of unity and harmony with God.

The idea of *Tikkun Olam* is also manifested in the practice of *Teshuvah* (repentance). Kabbalah sees repentance not only as a process of personal correction, but as a means of restoring spiritual harmony in the universe. When a person acknowledges their mistakes and commits to changing, they not only elevate their own soul, but also release energies that were trapped in the *Qlipot*. *Teshuvah* is seen as a way of transforming evil into good, redeeming past failures and converting them into opportunities for spiritual growth. Kabbalah teaches that, through sincere *Teshuvah*, even the deepest mistakes can be corrected and transformed into sources of light.

Another important practice in *Tikkun Olam* is the recitation of the Psalms. The Psalms are seen as sacred texts that contain spiritual power, and their recitation is considered a way of releasing divine light into the world. The Kabbalist can recite specific Psalms with the intention of bringing healing, protection, or spiritual elevation to themselves or others. The Psalms are also used in times of crisis or need, when the person seeks divine intervention to correct an imbalance or resolve a difficult situation. Each Psalm contains a spiritual code, and by reciting it with the proper *kavanah*, the practitioner helps to unblock the flow of divine energy that brings correction to the world.

Tikkun Olam also involves recognizing the impact of daily choices. Kabbalah teaches that every action, thought, and decision a person makes has cosmic repercussions. Human free will is a powerful gift, and every choice can contribute to the elevation or imbalance of the universe. The Kabbalist lives with the awareness that their decisions affect not only their own life, but also the world around them. By choosing to act with kindness, mercy, and justice, the individual directly contributes to *Tikkun Olam*, restoring the balance between the forces of light and darkness.

Another essential aspect of *Tikkun Olam* is collective work. Kabbalah teaches that the correction of the world is a shared responsibility of all humanity. Although each person has a unique role in the *Tikkun*, the process of correction cannot be carried out in isolation. The final *Tikkun* requires the collective effort of all, and each person, by elevating themselves spiritually, helps to elevate the world as a whole. This community aspect of *Tikkun Olam* is reflected in practices such as the collective study of the Torah, where the exchange of spiritual wisdom between individuals creates an atmosphere of collective elevation.

Tikkun Olam is deeply linked to the messianic vision of Kabbalah. The messianic era is seen as the moment when the *Tikkun* will be complete, and the entire universe will be restored to its original perfection. In the Kabbalistic view, the world is constantly moving towards this final correction, and each generation has the responsibility to accelerate this process. Although the final *Tikkun* is a cosmic event, Kabbalah teaches that each individual action, however small, contributes to bringing this era of light and harmony closer.

Thus, *Tikkun Olam* is not just a philosophical or abstract idea, but a spiritual and material practice that permeates all areas of life. From prayer and meditation to daily actions of kindness and justice, the Kabbalist actively participates in the correction of the world, aligning themselves with the divine purpose of restoring harmony and light in creation. *Tikkun Olam* is a continuous journey of growth and transformation, both personal and global, and Kabbalah teaches us that, through our active participation in this process, we can contribute to the elevation of all humanity and the universe.

Chapter 9
Reincarnation in Kabbalah

Reincarnation is a concept deeply explored in Kabbalah, being one of the keys to understanding the soul's journey through different lives and the experiences it undergoes. In the Kabbalistic view, the soul is not confined to a single physical existence but goes through various incarnations, repeatedly returning to the material world to complete its spiritual missions and correct the flaws accumulated in previous lives. This cycle of rebirth is known as *Gilgul* (reincarnation), and it is seen as part of the ongoing process of spiritual correction and evolution of the soul.

The central goal of reincarnation, in Kabbalah, is the pursuit of spiritual perfection. The soul is a divine spark, and its mission is to return to the source from which it came, which is God. However, during its journey through the physical and spiritual worlds, the soul accumulates imperfections and imbalances. This occurs due to incorrect actions, misdirected desires, or failures to complete the spiritual tasks assigned to each life. When a soul does not complete its mission in one existence, it is sent back to the physical world to try again, carrying with it the unlearned lessons and uncorrected errors.

The *Sefer HaGilgulim* (The Book of Reincarnations), attributed to the great Kabbalist Isaac Luria, the Arizal, is one of the most important works for understanding the concept of *Gilgul* in Kabbalah. In this text, Luria explains how the soul is composed of several parts, and how each part can be reincarnated independently to correct specific flaws. According to Luria, the soul has three main components: *Nefesh*, *Ruach*, and *Neshamah*. Each of these levels can be reincarnated separately, depending on what needs to be corrected. For example, the *Nefesh*, which is most connected to physical actions and desires, may need correction in one life, while the *Ruach*, which is related to emotions and morality, may require work in another.

Divine justice in reincarnation is also a central theme in Kabbalah. Souls that fail in their missions are not punished in a final way, but are given new opportunities to correct their flaws in future lives. This reflects the Kabbalistic view that God is essentially merciful and gives souls numerous chances for rectification. However, the process of reincarnation can be painful, as the soul is often placed in situations of challenge, suffering, or conflict that mirror its past mistakes. These challenges are not seen as punishments, but as opportunities for growth and rectification.

Each life is, therefore, a chapter in the story of a soul's evolution, and the events and circumstances that a person encounters are carefully orchestrated by Divine Providence to provide opportunities for learning and correction. Kabbalah teaches that nothing in a person's life is random. All encounters, difficulties, and joys have a deep spiritual purpose. The soul attracts to itself the experiences necessary for its growth and rectification. If a person repeatedly faces a certain type of challenge, this may be a sign that this area of life is where correction needs to happen.

Another essential aspect of reincarnation in Kabbalah is the idea of *Tikun*, or correction. A soul's personal *Tikun* is the set of spiritual tasks and corrections that it needs to accomplish in its various incarnations. Some souls have a light *Tikun*, meaning they have few corrections to make and their lives may be more harmonious. Others, however, carry a greater burden of flaws to be corrected and may face more difficult lives. Kabbalah teaches that, although the process of correction can be challenging, it is essential for the soul's spiritual growth.

A question frequently raised in the context of reincarnation is human suffering. Kabbalah offers a particular perspective on suffering, stating that it is often a necessary part of the process of spiritual correction. The pain and difficulties that a person faces in their current life may be the result of incorrect actions in a previous life, and are intended to correct those errors. This does not mean that suffering is a punishment, but rather a way of realigning the soul with its divine purpose.

Human relationships are also deeply influenced by the concept of reincarnation. Kabbalah teaches that souls often reincarnate in groups, meaning that friends, family, and even enemies from a previous life may reappear in new incarnations, playing different roles.

These relationships are opportunities for rectification and mutual growth. For example, a person may reincarnate in a specific family to correct a dysfunctional relationship from a past life, or to help another soul achieve its *Tikun*.

Another interesting aspect of reincarnation in Kabbalah is the idea of soul sharing. Kabbalah teaches that, in certain cases, a soul can be divided into several parts and reincarnated in different bodies simultaneously. This happens when a soul has many corrections to make and needs to be in more than one place at the same time to fulfill its *Tikun*. These "parts" of the soul may meet or cross paths in their incarnations, without knowing that they are part of the same original soul. This concept suggests that human connections are much deeper than they appear at first glance.

Reincarnation is also connected to *Tikun Olam*, the concept of universal correction discussed earlier. Just as individual souls need to go through a process of correction and elevation, the world as a whole is also in a continuous process of rectification. Each soul has a role to play in the collective correction, and by completing its own corrections, it contributes to the global correction. The messianic era, in the Kabbalistic view, is the time when all souls will have completed their corrections and the world will reach a state of harmony and perfection.

Furthermore, the concept of karma in Kabbalah is similar to, but distinct from, what is found in other spiritual traditions. The Hebrew term for this is *Schar VeOnesh* (reward and punishment). In Kabbalah, a person's actions in one life create spiritual consequences that need to be balanced in future lives. This can be compared to karma, but with a greater emphasis on correction and spiritual rectification, rather than just retribution. If a person failed to fulfill their spiritual obligations in one life, these tasks will be transferred to their future incarnations.

Kabbalah also offers techniques for identifying karmic patterns and learning from past lives. Although most people do not have conscious memories of their previous incarnations, Kabbalistic meditation can help access spiritual memories that reveal clues about a soul's *Tikun*. Some Kabbalists practice specific meditations to connect with these memories and understand the challenges and lessons their soul needs to face in this life. This may include meditations with the Divine Names, where the Kabbalist seeks guidance to understand the spiritual roots of their challenges.

Therefore, reincarnation in Kabbalah is a mechanism of learning and spiritual evolution. The soul is always in motion, returning to Earth to correct errors, learn lessons, and ultimately, to fully unite with the divine source. The concept of *Gilgul* offers a broader view of the soul's journey, helping us understand that each life is part of a much larger process of growth and correction. Every action, every thought, and every experience has a lasting impact on the soul, and by recognizing this, the Kabbalist can live with more purpose and awareness, knowing that their choices in this life have repercussions beyond the physical world and beyond their present existence.

Now that we understand the concept of reincarnation (*Gilgul*) and its function within the Kabbalistic cosmology, it is important to explore how to identify karmic patterns and memories of past lives, as well as how this knowledge can be applied in the process of spiritual elevation and the pursuit of completeness. Kabbalah not only teaches that the soul reincarnates to correct past flaws, but also offers methods to help the practitioner discover which aspects of their current life are related to previous experiences, allowing them to work more consciously and purposefully on their personal *Tikun*.

The process of identifying karmic patterns in current life is subtle and requires attention to recurring circumstances and challenges that arise repeatedly. Kabbalah teaches that, often, the problems we persistently face in our lives are echoes of unresolved imbalances or flaws from previous incarnations. If a person faces constant difficulties in a specific area – whether in relationships, health, finances, or spirituality – this may be an indication that the soul is dealing with issues that were not corrected in past lives.

A practical way to begin identifying these patterns is through conscious self-observation and regular reflection on the significant events that happen in life. Kabbalists suggest that the practitioner keep a spiritual diary, where they record not only daily events, but also the emotions and reactions that arise in response to these events. Over time, patterns may emerge, and the repetition of certain types of challenges or behaviors may be a sign of an unresolved *Tikun* from a previous incarnation.

In addition to self-observation, Kabbalistic meditation offers a powerful tool for exploring the spiritual roots of current challenges. By meditating on the *Sefirot*, for example, the Kabbalist can seek to understand which aspect of their soul is unbalanced and requires correction. If the person is experiencing continuous conflicts in their relationships, they can meditate on the *Sefirah* of *Tiferet*, which is associated with harmony, seeking insight on how to better integrate the forces of *Chesed* (mercy) and *Gevurah* (judgment). If the challenges are related to the ego or sense of purpose, meditation on *Yesod* or *Malchut* can bring clarity on how to align life with the correct spiritual energies.

Meditation on the Divine Names is another central practice in identifying karmic patterns. The 72 Names of God, which act as channels of spiritual energy, can be used to reveal information about the soul's purpose and the challenges it must overcome in its journey of correction. Each of these Names corresponds to a unique spiritual frequency, and by meditating on them, the practitioner can open their mind to insights about the nature of their spiritual mission. Meditation on the Name *Ayin Lamed Mem*, for example, is traditionally used to bring clarity about karma and help dispel illusions that prevent understanding of the personal *Tikun*.

In addition to meditations, Kabbalah teaches that dreams are a gateway to spiritual memories and past lives. Dreams, according to Kabbalistic tradition, are moments when the soul temporarily rises from the physical body and connects with the spiritual realms. During this separation, it is possible for the soul to access information from previous incarnations or receive messages about its current correction. By practicing Kabbalistic dream interpretation, the practitioner can begin to decipher the recurring symbols and themes in their dreams, identifying patterns that may be connected to their past lives.

One of the most practical methods to increase dream clarity is the recitation of specific prayers before sleep, combined with a focused intention. One of the recommended practices is to recite Psalm 91, which is seen as a spiritual protection and a way to prepare the soul to receive clear messages during the dream state. Another Kabbalistic technique involves meditating on the Tetragrammaton (YHVH) before sleep, visualizing the sacred letters illuminating the mind and spirit, asking for guidance and clarity about the challenges and *Tikun* of current life.

In addition to dreams, certain Kabbalists also suggest the use of spiritual amplifiers, such as amulets or Kabbalistic stones, which help to unlock access to spiritual memories. These amulets are engraved with Divine Names or combinations of Hebrew letters that create a field of protection around the soul, allowing it to receive spiritual information more clearly. However, it is important to emphasize that the power of these objects does not reside in their physical properties, but in the spiritual intention (*kavanah*) with which they are used.

Once the practitioner begins to identify the karmic patterns and understand the nature of their *Tikun*, the next step is to actively work on correcting these imbalances. Kabbalah offers a series of practices to help in the process of correction, from acts of *Tzedakah* (charity) to performing *Mitzvot* with focused intention. When a Kabbalist discovers that they have a pattern of lack of generosity or selfishness from past lives, they can intensify their practice of *Tzedakah*, not only as an act of charity, but as a way to correct a spiritual aspect that has become unbalanced.

In addition to the *Mitzvot*, Kabbalistic repentance (*Teshuvah*) is a fundamental practice for correcting past mistakes. *Teshuvah*, as we have seen, is not just a process of asking for forgiveness, but a profound transformation of the soul, which allows the practitioner to reorient their life towards the divine light. Through *Teshuvah*, the Kabbalist not only corrects their mistakes, but also transcends the limitations of their previous incarnations, elevating themselves spiritually.

Teshuvah involves four main stages: sincere repentance for the mistakes made, the commitment to change, the verbal confession of the mistakes (usually through prayer), and finally, the rectification of the actions through concrete changes in daily life. This process not only releases the practitioner from accumulated negative karma, but also transforms negative energy into positive, since the mistake made becomes an opportunity for growth and spiritual elevation.

An advanced practice within Kabbalah for working with personal *Tikun* is meditation on reincarnation. Certain Kabbalists recommend meditating on the concept of *Gilgul* as a way to recognize that the soul is in a continuous cycle of learning and evolution. During this meditation, the practitioner visualizes their soul as a spark of light moving through the different spheres of existence, clearing flaws, accumulating wisdom, and constantly returning to the physical world for new opportunities for correction. This brings a broader and deeper perspective on the spiritual journey, helping the Kabbalist to accept the challenges of life as part of a larger process of elevation.

Another way to work with reincarnation is through the practice of mindful care in interpersonal relationships. Kabbalah teaches that many of our interactions with other people, especially the most intense or conflictive ones, are reflections of karmic connections from past lives. If a relationship is particularly challenging, the Kabbalist can approach the situation with the awareness that this person may have played an important role in a previous life and that the current interaction offers an opportunity for mutual correction. The practice of forgiveness, both for oneself and for others, is seen as one of the most powerful ways to release accumulated negative karma.

Finally, the Kabbalistic wisdom about reincarnation invites the practitioner to live with an expanded awareness of the spiritual purpose of each life.

Understanding that we are in a continuous cycle of correction and learning not only helps us face challenges with more patience and wisdom, but also encourages us to act with more responsibility in our daily actions and choices. Each life is a precious opportunity for spiritual advancement, and each choice has repercussions that extend beyond the present existence.

By recognizing the depth of personal *Tikun*, Kabbalah teaches us to become conscious co-creators of our spiritual destiny, actively participating in the correction of past flaws and preparing our soul for completeness and final union with the divine. Reincarnation is not just a cycle of repetition; it is an upward spiral of growth and spiritual realization, in which each incarnation brings new opportunities for correction, purification, and elevation of the soul.

Chapter 10
The Secret Language of Kabbalah
Gematria

Gematria is one of the most enigmatic and fascinating tools of Kabbalah, used to unveil the hidden meanings of sacred texts, revealing profound layers of spiritual wisdom that are encoded in letters and numbers. At its core, Gematria is a system of Kabbalistic numerology that assigns numerical values to Hebrew letters, allowing the scholar to find spiritual correspondences between seemingly unrelated words, phrases, and concepts. Through this system, the Kabbalist is able to access a secret and symbolic language, where numbers become portals to higher spiritual realities.

In the Hebrew alphabet, each letter has a corresponding numerical value, and this allows words to be analyzed in terms of their summed numerical values. For example, the letter Alef (א) has a value of 1, Bet (ב) has a value of 2, and so on, up to the value of 400, which corresponds to the letter Tav (ת). Gematria is not just a mathematical exercise, but a tool that reveals the spiritual connections between words and ideas. By adding up the numerical values of the letters in a word, the Kabbalist can discover other words or phrases with the same value, suggesting a mystical connection between the concepts they represent.

A classic and frequently cited example in Gematria is the relationship between the words Echad (אחד), which means "one" or "unity," and Ahavah (אהבה), which means "love." Both words add up to 13, and when two times 13 are added together (representing the reciprocity of love between two parties), the result is 26, the numerical value of the Tetragrammaton (YHVH), the Divine Name of God. This example reveals that love (Ahavah) is the key to experiencing divine unity (Echad) and that, by living in love, we connect more deeply with the presence of God.

Gematria has its roots in ancient texts of the Jewish tradition, such as the Sefer Yetzirah and the Zohar, and was extensively developed by great Kabbalists like the Arizal (Isaac Luria) and the Ramban (Nachmanides). These sages believed that the Hebrew alphabet is not just a set of linguistic symbols, but the fundamental letters of creation, used by God to form the universe. In Kabbalah, God's very act of creating the world is seen as a linguistic process, where Hebrew letters act as building blocks of reality. Each letter carries a specific spiritual energy, and the combination of these letters into words forms a mystical code that reveals the secrets of creation.

The use of Gematria is especially important in the interpretation of sacred texts, such as the Torah, where each word, and even each letter, is seen as possessing multiple meanings. Through Gematria, the Kabbalist can find numerical correspondences between different passages of the Torah and other sacred texts, revealing spiritual connections that are not apparent in the literal reading. This method of deep interpretation helps the scholar to access the esoteric layers of the texts and to understand the hidden meaning behind the words.

There are several types of Gematria used in Kabbalah, each with its own rules and variations. The most common and basic form is called Gematria Peshutah (simple Gematria), where Hebrew letters are assigned their standard numerical values. In addition, there is also Gematria Katan (reduced Gematria), where the numerical values are reduced to a single digit. For example, the letter Tav (400) would be reduced to 4, the letter Mem (40) would be reduced to 4, and so on. This form of Gematria is used to simplify calculations and reveal new levels of correspondence between words.

Another type of Gematria is Gematria Milui (full Gematria), where the numerical value of a letter is calculated not only based on the letter itself, but also on the letters that make it up when spelled out. For example, the letter Alef (א), which normally has a value of 1, would be written as Alef-Lamed-Peh (אלף), with a total numerical value of 111 (1 + 30 + 80). Through Gematria Milui, the Kabbalist can discover additional layers of meaning in letters and words, exploring the different aspects of spiritual reality that are encoded in their expanded forms.

The study of Gematria is not limited to understanding words and letters, but also encompasses time and space. Kabbalah teaches that cycles of time, such as years, months, and days, also have numerical correspondences that can be analyzed to reveal the spiritual purpose of specific events and eras. For example, the numerical value of the word Shanah (הנש), which means "year," is 355, which refers to the lunar cycle of 355 days. This suggests a connection between the concept of time and the movement of celestial bodies, revealing a cosmic harmony that underlies creation.

Gematria is widely used in proper names, especially in choosing names for children. In Kabbalah, it is believed that a person's name contains the spiritual destiny and purpose of their soul. When choosing a name, Kabbalists often consult Gematria to ensure that the numerical value of the name is in harmony with the child's spiritual goals. In addition, Gematria can be used to analyze names in relation to important events in a person's life, such as weddings or births, helping to identify specific spiritual qualities associated with those moments.

Another classic example of the use of Gematria is the correspondence between the word Mashiach (חישמ), which means "Messiah," and the word Nachash (שחנ), which means "serpent." Both words add up to 358. This equivalence reveals the spiritual duality present in the concept of redemption. While the Mashiach represents redemption and the correction of the world, the Nachash symbolizes evil and sin, the serpent that caused the fall of Adam and Eve in the Garden of Eden. This correspondence suggests that by overcoming the forces of evil (Nachash), the world can open itself to the arrival of the Mashiach, completing the Tikun Olam (correction of the world).

Gematria is also linked to free will and spiritual karma. The Kabbalist understands that the choices we make in life have spiritual correspondences, and that our names, actions, and thoughts create a numerical resonance in the universe. Through Gematria, it is possible to identify these energies and work actively to balance them. If a person faces spiritual challenges or imbalances, Gematria can be used to identify which areas of life are in disharmony and which words or numerical combinations can help restore spiritual balance.

A practical application of Gematria in the daily life of the Kabbalist is in meditation on sacred words and numbers. By focusing their mind on a specific word and its numerical value, the Kabbalist can enter a meditative state that allows them to connect with the spiritual energies associated with that word. For example, meditating on the number 26, which is the numerical value of the Divine Name YHVH, helps to bring awareness to the presence of God and the unity of creation. Similarly, meditating on the number 18, which corresponds to the word Chai (חי), meaning "life," can be a powerful practice for attracting energies of vitality and spiritual growth.

Gematria is more than a mystical system of numbers; it is a living spiritual language that allows the Kabbalist to penetrate the secrets of the universe and uncover the hidden connections that permeate reality. By studying Gematria, the Kabbalist discovers that everything in the universe is interconnected through numerical codes, and that these codes contain the key to understanding the divine will and the purpose of creation. Each number, each letter, and each word carries within it an infinity of spiritual meanings that, once revealed, help the practitioner to align with divine energies and find their way on the spiritual journey.

Now that we have explored the foundations of Gematria and how it can be used to reveal deep spiritual connections between words and concepts, it is time to delve into the practical applications of this tool in Kabbalistic study and daily life. Gematria offers the practitioner a way to understand and influence the reality around them, through the transformative power of Hebrew numbers and letters.

One of the first steps to working with Gematria is the use of numerical meditations. Meditation on sacred words and numbers is a practice that helps to bring spiritual insights and to tune the mind to the divine energies associated with certain numerical values. A simple exercise to start with is to choose an important word, such as the Divine Name YHVH (הוהי), which has the numerical value of 26. By meditating on this number, the practitioner can visualize the letters and allow their meaning and energy to fill the mind, bringing a sense of unity with the divine.

This exercise can be expanded by incorporating Gematria Milui, where the letters are written in their full form. For example, YHVH (הוהי) can be expressed as Yod-Vav-Dalet (דוי), Heh-Alef (הא), Vav-Alef-Vav (ואו), Heh-Alef (אה), which raises the total numerical value to

72. Meditating on this expanded form of the Divine Name can open new channels of spiritual perception, revealing the complexity and depth of the divine energy that permeates the universe. This meditation helps to strengthen the connection with higher spiritual energies and can be used for mental clarity, spiritual healing, or protection.

Another practical technique involves Gematria applied to the analysis of names. Since Kabbalah teaches that people's names carry their spiritual destiny, Gematria can be used to discover the soul's purpose through a person's name. To do this, the practitioner begins by calculating the numerical value of the person's full name in Hebrew. Then, they look for other words or phrases with the same numerical value, in order to discover which qualities or spiritual challenges are associated with that person.

For example, if a person's name has the numerical value of 248, the Kabbalist may observe that this value corresponds to the word Rachum (מוחר), which means "compassionate." This may suggest that the person's spiritual mission involves developing the quality of compassion in their interactions. In addition, 248 is the number of positive Mitzvot (commandments that command doing something), which could indicate that this soul has a strong inclination to perform positive and spiritually uplifting actions. This type of analysis offers practical insights into the nature and spiritual challenges that a person faces, helping them to live in a way that is more aligned with their Tikun.

An even deeper practice is the use of Gematria to interpret events in a person's life. Kabbalists believe that events are not accidental, and that important events, such as the birth of a child, weddings, or even life crises, have hidden spiritual meanings that can be discovered through Gematria. An exercise for this is to calculate the numerical value of the date of a significant event and then look for words or concepts with the same numerical value. This can offer a broader understanding of the spiritual purpose behind the event.

For example, if a person was born on a date whose numerical value is equivalent to 613, the number of the Mitzvot of the Torah, this may suggest that this person's life is deeply connected with the observance and fulfillment of the divine commandments. The analysis of Gematria applied to important events can help the person understand karmic patterns, revealing spiritual lessons that are being offered through their life experiences.

Gematria can also be used for prayer and meditation, especially when focusing on certain numbers or words that have a specific spiritual energy. One of the traditional methods is to meditate on the number 18, which corresponds to the word Chai (חי), meaning "life." By focusing on this number during meditation, the practitioner can attract energies of vitality and renewal. This meditation can be useful in times of stagnation or when the practitioner wishes to bring more energy and spiritual growth into their life.

Another significant number in Kabbalistic meditation is 45, which is the numerical value of Adam

(םדא), the first human being, and is also associated with the Sephirah of Tiferet, which represents harmony and balance. Meditating on the number 45 can help the practitioner find inner harmony, balancing the opposing forces of mercy and severity, and integrating these energies into their daily life. By harmonizing these forces, the person aligns with the greater purpose of spiritual balance, both within themselves and in their relationships with others.

In addition to meditations and prayers, Gematria can be used in concrete actions to generate specific spiritual results. A classic example is the practice of Tzedakah (charity). In the Kabbalistic tradition, there is a custom of donating amounts of money that correspond to certain significant numbers in Gematria. For example, giving 18 units of currency (a value equivalent to "life") can be seen as an act of donating vitality, helping both the receiver and the giver to connect with the energies of renewal and spiritual growth.

Another Kabbalistic practice that uses Gematria is the use of amulets and talismans. Certain Divine Names or combinations of Hebrew letters are engraved on amulets or pieces of jewelry for spiritual protection, healing, or prosperity. These amulets are created based on Gematria calculations that connect the wearer to specific energies of the universe. For example, amulets that contain the Name El Shaddai (ידש לא), whose numerical value is 345, are often used for protection, as this Name of God is associated with security and the ability to overcome adverse forces.

Gematria can also be applied in the reading and interpretation of the Torah, helping the practitioner to unveil the deeper levels of hidden meanings in the sacred texts. When studying a verse of the Torah, the Kabbalist can calculate the numerical value of specific words or phrases and look for other passages with the same value. This reveals spiritual correspondences between different parts of the Torah that, at first glance, do not seem to be connected. For example, the numerical value of the word Bereshit (בְּרֵאשִׁית), which means "in the beginning," is 913. This numerical value can be associated with other words or concepts in the sacred text, revealing new layers of meaning.

The use of Gematria to interpret sacred texts is a form of deep and esoteric study. Many Kabbalists believe that each letter, word, and number in the Torah contains spiritual secrets that can be revealed through this method. By studying Gematria, the practitioner develops the ability to see beyond the surface level of the text, accessing the Sod (esoteric) and Remez (symbolic) levels of interpretation, where the spiritual mysteries of creation and divine purpose are revealed.

One of the simplest exercises to start applying Gematria in reading the Torah is to choose a specific verse and calculate the numerical value of a central word. Then, the practitioner can search for words with the same numerical value in other passages of the Torah or in Kabbalistic texts. This practice helps to build a network of spiritual connections between different ideas, showing how Kabbalah views reality as an interconnected whole, where each part reflects the whole.

Gematria is, ultimately, a tool of spiritual revelation. It is not just a system of numbers, but a way of understanding the spiritual energies that sustain the universe. Through it, the Kabbalist is able to access hidden levels of wisdom and bring that wisdom into their daily life in a practical and transformative way. Whether through meditation, study, or action, Gematria connects the individual to the depths of divine mysteries, helping them to find their purpose and align with the highest spiritual energies.

Chapter 11
Evil and Free Will in Kabbalah

Within Kabbalah, the concept of evil occupies a central place in the spiritual development of the soul and the purpose of creation. Unlike more traditional views that see evil as something to be destroyed or eradicated, Kabbalah teaches us that evil has a necessary function in the cosmos. It is a force that, when understood and mastered, becomes a catalyst for spiritual growth and the manifestation of free will. Evil, in the Kabbalistic view, is deeply connected to the concept of darkness and concealment, and its existence enables human beings to make conscious choices, allowing free will to flourish as an instrument of spiritual elevation.

The creation of evil is related to the contraction or Tzimtzum, one of the most profound concepts in Kabbalah, introduced by Isaac Luria, the Arizal. Before creation, there was only the infinite light of God, a light so intense that it left no room for the existence of anything besides itself. To allow for the creation of a world with free will and autonomy, God needed to "conceal" part of His light, creating a void where independent existence could occur. In this space, physical reality and human souls began to exist, but this contraction also gave rise to a condition of spiritual darkness, where the divine presence becomes less evident. This darkness is the fertile ground where evil can arise, but it is also where the potential for free will is planted.

Evil, in Kabbalah, is described as a chaotic energy, a force that is out of balance with the divine purpose, but which is still part of creation. It manifests in various forms, both in the external world, such as wars and destruction, and in the internal world, through selfish impulses, pride, and unrestrained desire. However, its presence in the world is seen as temporary and necessary, as it challenges human beings to choose between good and evil, between light and darkness. Evil offers a choice that, when overcome, leads to spiritual growth and the elevation of the soul.

This choice is at the heart of the Kabbalistic concept of free will (Bechirah Chofshit). Kabbalah teaches that free will is the soul's ability to consciously choose to follow the path of light, that is, to align with the divine will, or to follow the path of darkness, which aligns with the ego and unrestrained material desire. Free will is considered one of the most precious gifts that God gave to humanity, as it allows each individual to actively participate in creation, becoming a co-creator in the process of correcting and elevating the world.

The struggle between good and evil in Kabbalah is also represented in the opposing forces that permeate creation. At their origin, these forces are present in the Sefirot, the ten divine emanations that govern the universe. Two of these Sefirot, Chesed (kindness) and Gevurah (severity), exemplify this tension between opposing forces. While Chesed represents unconditional love and expansion, Gevurah brings the energy of judgment and restriction. Both are necessary for the balance of the universe, but when Gevurah becomes excessive, manifestations of evil arise – severe judgment, suffering, and separation. On the other hand, an imbalance of Chesed can lead to chaos and a lack of boundaries. The balance between these forces is what allows for harmony and spiritual growth.

Free will can only be truly exercised in a world where evil exists, for it is through the conscious choice between light and darkness that human beings can grow spiritually. If there were no evil, the choice for good would be automatic and without merit. Thus, evil is a force that gives human beings the opportunity to transcend their own nature. When a person resists the temptations of the ego, they transform the darkness of evil into light, thus fulfilling the spiritual purpose of their soul.

Kabbalah teaches that the human soul is composed of different layers, each with its own relationship to good and evil. The lowest level of the soul, called Nefesh, is most connected to physical desires and basic emotions. This is the entry point of evil into human consciousness, where the ego and material desire can overshadow the soul's connection to the divine. However, as a person works spiritually, they can elevate their soul to higher levels, such as Ruach and Neshamah, which are more connected to morality, spiritual intuition, and divine wisdom. The higher the soul, the greater the ability to discern between good and evil, and the greater the power to consciously choose to follow the path of light.

The Torah and Kabbalistic teachings offer guidance on how to master the forces of evil and awaken the potential of free will. The practice of Mitzvot, the divine commandments, is one of the central means to keep the soul aligned with good and away from the negative influence of evil. By fulfilling the commandments with intention and spiritual focus, the individual strengthens their connection to the divine light and weakens the forces of darkness that can arise through the ego and material desires.

Another important aspect of evil in Kabbalah is the concept of Sitra Achra, which means "the other side." Sitra Achra refers to the spiritual dimension where evil and darkness dwell. These forces are seen as part of the divine system, but in a state of imbalance and distance from the light. Evil, according to this view, is not an independent force, but rather a state of disconnection from the divine source. The spiritual work of the Kabbalist is to transform the Sitra Achra into light, bringing balance and harmony to the universe.

Kabbalah also teaches us that free will can be strengthened through meditation and spiritual reflection. By meditating on the opposing energies of Chesed and Gevurah, the Kabbalist learns to recognize the forces of good and evil within themselves and in the world around them. Through meditation, they cultivate the ability to make conscious choices that bring them closer to good and away from negative influences. In addition, reflection on one's own actions and intentions is an essential practice for developing free will and discerning the correct path to follow.

A classic example in Kabbalah that illustrates the struggle between good and evil is the story of Adam and Eve in the Garden of Eden. The original sin is seen as the first example of free will exercised incorrectly, where Adam and Eve yielded to the temptations of the serpent (a representation of evil) and disobeyed the divine command. However, Kabbalah teaches that even this act of disobedience was not entirely negative, as it brought to the world the possibility of correction and elevation. Through the wrong choices of Adam and Eve, humanity was introduced to the concept of Tikkun, the spiritual correction that is achieved by transforming evil into good and darkness into light.

Kabbalah reminds us that evil is not eternal. It exists as part of the process of spiritual elevation and correction, but it will eventually be overcome. The messianic era, or Olam HaBa (the world to come), is seen as the time when evil will be completely transformed and humanity will live in a state of unity and harmony with God. In this vision, evil will not be destroyed, but rather integrated and transformed into a new source of light and spiritual growth.

As we discussed earlier, Kabbalah understands evil as a necessary force for creation, offering human beings the opportunity to exercise free will. The existence of evil is not an end in itself, but a spiritual challenge that allows us to consciously choose good and elevate ourselves spiritually. Now, let's explore how to apply these concepts in a practical way in everyday life, with the aim of overcoming the temptations and spiritual challenges we encounter, using free will as a tool for growth and inner transformation.

Kabbalistic practice teaches that recognizing the forces of evil within us is the first step to mastering them. These forces are not external, but manifest in our selfish desires, inclinations to negativity, and impulses that distance us from our divine essence. Kabbalah identifies these negative inclinations as the Yetzer Hara, or evil inclination, which exists in opposition to the Yetzer Hatov, the good inclination. This internal dualism reflects the cosmic tension between light and darkness, but it also opens a path for spiritual growth, because every time we resist the Yetzer Hara, we advance in our journey of spiritual correction, the Tikkun.

One of the most important Kabbalistic tools for dealing with inner evil is the concept of Hitbonenut, or deep reflection. This practice involves setting aside daily moments to examine our thoughts, emotions, and actions. Reflection is not just a mental analysis, but a spiritual meditation on our motivations and decisions, questioning whether we are acting from the Yetzer Hara or the Yetzer Hatov. Through Hitbonenut, the Kabbalist can identify patterns of behavior that are dominated by negative impulses and then make more conscious decisions that align them with good.

A useful technique in this practice of reflection is daily self-analysis through a spiritual journal, where one records the moments in which we faced moral challenges and how we reacted to them. The Kabbalist can then examine these records, looking for patterns where the Yetzer Hara took control and reflecting on how they could have acted differently. This practice helps to strengthen free will, because by becoming aware of our weaknesses, we better prepare ourselves to act with more clarity and purpose in future situations.

In addition to reflection, Kabbalah teaches that corrective actions are essential for overcoming the forces of evil. Every time we resist a temptation or act in accordance with good, we transform a portion of darkness into light. This can be practiced in small daily acts, such as controlling words spoken impulsively, overcoming feelings of anger, or choosing to be generous when the ego pushes us to selfishness. These small victories are crucial in the spiritual battle, as each act of overcoming strengthens our soul and connects us more deeply with the divine light.

The practice of Mitzvot (commandments) also plays a crucial role in overcoming evil and spiritual elevation. In Kabbalah, Mitzvot are seen not only as religious obligations, but as channels for bringing light into the world and elevating the soul. Fulfilling the Mitzvot with conscious intention (Kavanah) connects us to the divine will, helping us to overcome the temptations of the Yetzer Hara. For example, the regular practice of Tzedakah (charity) is an act that refines the ego and purifies the soul, transforming the desire for self-aggrandizement into an act of altruism and kindness.

Another important aspect of Kabbalah is the concept of active resistance to evil, which involves techniques to block the influence of negative forces in our lives. These forces, known as Klipot (husks or shells), are manifestations of chaotic energies that envelop the soul and divert it from its spiritual purpose. Klipot can arise from our own negative behaviors, such as pride, envy, lust, or greed, and they keep us trapped in a cycle of spiritual darkness. To break free from these forces, the Kabbalist uses practices such as meditation and the invocation of Divine Names.

Meditation on the 72 Names of God, for example, is a powerful practice that helps to dissipate the energy of the Klipot. Each of the 72 Names is composed of three Hebrew letters, which form a sequence of sounds and spiritual vibrations. It is believed that by meditating on these Names, the practitioner connects directly with the divine energies that can neutralize negative influences and bring balance to the soul. An example is the Name Ayin Lamed Mem, which is used to dispel confusion and bring mental clarity, an important tool when we are confronted with decisions that involve a choice between good and evil.

Furthermore, the Kabbalistic practice of Teshuvah (repentance) is one of the most transformative tools in the fight against evil. Teshuvah, literally "return," involves a deep process of returning to the divine essence after having committed an error or sin. In the Kabbalistic view, sin is not just a moral transgression, but a distancing from the divine light. Through Teshuvah, the person recognizes their error, seeks to repair it, and, most importantly, transforms the negative energy resulting from that error into a new positive force.

Teshuvah involves three stages: sincere repentance, commitment to change, and corrective action. True repentance is recognizing the impact of our negative actions on our soul and on the world around us. Commitment to change requires a clear decision not to repeat the error, while corrective action may involve both repairing the damage caused and engaging in spiritually uplifting acts. Kabbalah sees the process of Teshuvah as one of the greatest divine gifts, as it offers the opportunity not only to fix what was broken, but also to rise to a higher spiritual state than before the error.

In addition to internal practices, Kabbalah also emphasizes the importance of community actions in combating evil. Building a society based on justice, kindness, and altruism is a way to weaken the negative forces that exist in the world. The concept of Tikkun Olam (correction of the world) involves both personal and collective correction. By acting for the benefit of others, we actively participate in the Kabbalistic mission of correcting the world and dissipating the energies of evil that affect both the individual and society.

Finally, Kabbalah teaches that conscious choice is the key to liberation from evil. Free will gives us the power to transform our reality by choosing good, even in the face of temptations and challenges. With each choice we make towards the light, we advance in our spiritual journey, transforming the world around us. Evil, therefore, is not an enemy to be destroyed, but a force to be transcended, an energy that, when redirected, can become a source of light and growth.

In challenging situations, such as when we face temptation, anger, or despair, an effective Kabbalistic practice is the conscious pause. Instead of reacting impulsively, the Kabbalist is taught to stop, breathe, and ask themselves, "Am I acting according to the Yetzer Hara or the Yetzer Hatov?" This simple reflection can transform a situation of potential darkness into an opportunity to act with wisdom and elevate the spirit.

Thus, the practice of Kabbalah in relation to evil and free will is not a rejection or denial of evil, but a path of transformation. By exercising our free will in a conscious way and aligned with spiritual teachings, we can transform negative energies into positive ones, thus fulfilling our role in Tikkun Olam.

Chapter 12
Cabalistic Healing and the Sefirot

In Kabbalah, healing is seen as a profound and multidimensional process, involving not only the physical body but also the spirit and soul. Kabbalistic healing is intrinsically linked to the Tree of Life and its ten Sefirot, which represent different aspects of divine existence and the manifestation of God in the world. Each Sefirah emanates a specific energy that can influence not only spiritual health but also the mental and physical health of human beings. Kabbalah teaches us that harmony between the Sefirot is essential for overall well-being, and that imbalances in the energies of these emanations can result in illness or suffering. Therefore, Kabbalistic healing seeks to restore the balance between these divine forces, providing internal and external harmony.

The Tree of Life can be seen as a spiritual map that describes the flow of divine energy from the supreme source, called Ein Sof (the Infinite), to the physical world. The Sefirot are the ten emanations or manifestations of this energy, which descend in a hierarchical process to create and sustain all existence. Each of the Sefirot has its own characteristics and qualities, and these qualities can be applied to

Kabbalistic healing, both on an individual and collective level.

Kabbalistic healing begins with the understanding that illness or suffering arises when there is an imbalance or blockage in the flow of energies of the Sefirot. When the natural flow of divine energies is interrupted, this affects the human being on different levels – physical, emotional, and spiritual. The goal of healing is to restore the balance between the Sefirot, allowing divine energy to flow freely again, bringing healing and harmony to all aspects of life.

Each of the ten Sefirot plays an important role in the healing process. Let's explore some of the main Sefirot and their connections to spiritual, mental, and physical well-being:

Keter (Crown) – Keter is the highest Sefirah of the Tree of Life, representing the divine will and the direct connection to the Ein Sof. In the context of healing, Keter is associated with higher wisdom and pure intention. The healing that emanates from Keter is of a high spiritual nature and is related to the ability to connect with the divine purpose of the soul. Imbalances in Keter can manifest as a lack of spiritual direction or a feeling of disconnection from life's purpose. Healing here involves alignment with the divine will and reconnection with the source.

Chokhmah (Wisdom) and Binah (Understanding) – These two Sefirot represent the intellectual aspect of creation and are the main sources of inspiration and spiritual insight. Chokhmah is the spark of divine inspiration, while Binah is the ability to process and understand this wisdom. Imbalances in these Sefirot can manifest as mental confusion, anxiety, or an inability to make clear decisions. Healing involves strengthening the connection with spiritual intuition and the ability to process this intuition in a practical way.

Chesed (Kindness) and Gevurah (Strength) – Chesed and Gevurah represent the emotional forces of expansive kindness and restrictive severity, respectively. The balance between these forces is essential for emotional health. Imbalances in Chesed can lead to excessive indulgence or a lack of boundaries, while imbalances in Gevurah can result in emotional rigidity, fear, or severe self-judgment. Healing here involves finding the balance between giving and receiving, between unconditional love and healthy restraint.

Tiferet (Beauty) – Tiferet is the central harmony of the Tree of Life, where the energy of Chesed and Gevurah meet in perfect balance. Tiferet is associated with physical and emotional healing, as it is the point where expansive love and restrictive force merge to create harmony. Imbalances in Tiferet can manifest as physical illnesses or emotional suffering. Healing through Tiferet involves seeking inner balance, bringing harmony to emotions, body, and spirit.

Netzach (Eternity) and Hod (Splendor) – Netzach and Hod are responsible for actions and reactions, representing persistence and humility, respectively. Netzach is the force that drives us forward, while Hod teaches us submission and acceptance. Imbalances in Netzach can lead to stubbornness or excessive ego, while imbalances in Hod can manifest as insecurity or passivity. Healing here involves finding the balance between self-confidence and humility, allowing actions to be guided by spiritual purpose, and not by selfish impulses.

Yesod (Foundation) – Yesod is the Sefirah that connects the spiritual world with the physical world, being responsible for the communication and integration of spiritual energies in our daily reality. Imbalances in Yesod can manifest as relational problems, emotional blockages, or psychological instability. Healing through Yesod involves restoring the flow of energy between spirit and body, facilitating emotional healing and strengthening relationships.

Malkhut (Kingdom) – Malkhut is the Sefirah that represents the physical world and our ability to manifest divine energy in material reality. Imbalances in Malkhut can result in physical illnesses, a lack of vital energy, or an inability to realize spiritual purposes in practical life. Healing here involves grounding spiritual energies in everyday life, allowing the body and mind to be aligned with the divine will.

Kabbalistic healing involves working with the energies of these Sefirot, both individually and together, to restore the flow of energy and bring balance to the spiritual system. Kabbalah offers various techniques and practices to facilitate this healing process, including meditation on the Sefirot, spiritual visualization, and the use of specific prayers and invocations that attract the healing energies of the Sefirot.

A common practice of Kabbalistic healing is meditation on the Tree of Life. In this meditation, the practitioner visualizes each Sefirah as a sphere of bright light, connected to the other Sefirot by channels of energy. The goal of the meditation is to visualize the uninterrupted flow of energy passing from one Sefirah to another, correcting any blockages or imbalances. For example, if a person is facing physical health problems, they can focus on the Sefirah of Tiferet, the source of balance and harmony, and visualize it radiating healing light to the body.

Another healing method involves the use of specific mantras and prayers, which are based on the Divine Names associated with each Sefirah. These Names are considered portals of energy that allow the practitioner to access the spiritual force of the corresponding Sefirah. Reciting these Names with concentrated intention helps to unlock the spiritual energies needed for healing and restoration of balance. For example, the Divine Name associated with Chesed is El (לא), and reciting this Name in meditation can help increase the energy of kindness and expansive healing.

Furthermore, Kabbalah teaches that healing is not just an individual process, but that it can also be achieved through service to others. By practicing acts of kindness and compassion, a person activates the energy of Chesed, which brings healing not only to themselves but to the world around them. The idea of Tikkun Olam (correction of the world) also applies to Kabbalistic healing, for as we heal ourselves, we contribute to global healing, restoring harmony in the physical and spiritual world.

Kabbalistic healing requires an integrated approach, involving meditation, visualization, prayer, and conscious action. Each practice is aligned with the energies of the Sefirot, facilitating the flow of these healing forces in the practitioner's life. Kabbalah teaches us that it is not enough just to understand the spiritual structure of the Tree of Life; it is necessary to actively and consciously incorporate these energies into our daily lives to achieve lasting and meaningful healing.

Meditation on the Sefirot for Healing

One of the most direct ways to access the healing energies of the Sefirot is through meditation. Here, we describe a simple yet powerful exercise that can be practiced regularly to restore energetic balance and promote inner healing:

Meditation Exercise on the Tree of Life:

Sit in a quiet place, with your spine straight and your eyes closed.

Take a few deep breaths to calm your mind and body.

Begin to visualize the Tree of Life in front of you, with its ten Sefirot shining like spheres of light.

Concentrate on each Sefirah, starting with Keter (at the top of the head) and descending to Malkhut (at the base of the spine).

At each Sefirah, visualize a bright light and feel the associated energetic quality. For example:

In Keter, feel the connection with divine will and the purpose of your soul.

In Tiferet, feel the energy of harmony and balance restoring physical and emotional health.

In Yesod, visualize the light flowing into your physical body, integrating spiritual energy and healing blockages.

As the light flows through each Sefirah, imagine that the areas of the body related to these emanations are being healed and revitalized.

Remain in this state of connection for a few minutes, absorbing the healing energy and letting it circulate throughout your body.

End the meditation by thanking the divine source for the healing received and feel yourself renewed.

This meditation can be practiced daily, or whenever the practitioner feels that there is an energetic imbalance or a health problem that needs to be addressed. Visualization of the Tree of Life helps connect the soul to the natural flow of divine energies, allowing the balance between the Sefirot to be restored.

Healing Through Divine Names

Divine Names are seen in Kabbalah as portals that channel specific energies from the spiritual world. Each Sefirah has an associated Name of God, and these Names can be invoked in prayers or meditations to bring healing and harmony.

Here are some examples of Divine Names linked to the Sefirot, and how to use them for healing:

Chesed (Kindness): The Divine Name associated with Chesed is El (לא). This Name is invoked to increase the energy of love and expansive healing.

Practice: While meditating or praying, visualize the bright white light of Chesed and recite the Name "El" repeatedly, feeling that kindness and healing are expanding to the entire body and soul. This is especially effective for those who suffer from a lack of emotional energy or are dealing with feelings of closure or isolation.

Gevurah (Strength): The Divine Name of Gevurah is Elohim (מיהולא), which represents justice and balance. Invoking this Name can help restore inner strength and emotional clarity.

Practice: Recite "Elohim" while visualizing a red light around your body, protecting you and strengthening your ability to discern and establish healthy boundaries. This can be especially useful for those who feel they are facing emotional challenges, such as fear or anxiety, or when it is necessary to restore self-control.

Tiferet (Beauty and Harmony): The Divine Name of Tiferet is YHVH Eloah Va'Da'at (תעדו הולא הוהי). This name is used to bring the body and spirit into harmony, and balance together mercy with judgment.

Practice: Recite the name while visualising a golden light eminating from the center of the chest (where Tiferet is located) and expanding through the whole body. This exercise is ideal for those who need physical and emotional healing, and it can bring internal peace and balance.

Specific Visualizations for Healing

Visualization is a powerful practice within Kabbalistic healing. By visualizing the Sefirot or the flows of spiritual energy, the practitioner creates a healing channel between the divine world and the physical world. Below are some practical visualizations that can be used for different types of healing:

Physical Healing: Visualize the Sefirah of Tiferet in the center of your body, like a golden sphere of light. Feel this light radiate to all parts of the body that need healing. Imagine this light dissolving energetic blockages and restoring health and physical balance. As the light expands, it heals cells, tissues, and organs, revitalizing the entire body with vital energy.

Emotional Healing: When facing an emotional imbalance, such as anxiety, sadness, or anger, visualize the Sefirah of Chesed on the right side of your body, radiating a soft white light. This light of kindness and compassion flows to the heart, calming disturbed emotions and bringing a sense of peace and acceptance. At the same time, visualize the light of Gevurah on the left side, bringing the strength needed to restore self-control and emotional clarity.

Spiritual Healing: To restore the connection with divine purpose or heal a spiritual crisis, visualize the Sefirah of Keter at the top of the head, shining like a crown of light. Imagine this divine light flowing down, filling the body with a pure white energy, connecting you directly to the Ein Sof (the Infinite). This practice helps restore a sense of purpose and spiritual clarity, as well as strengthen the connection with the divine.

Healing Through Mitzvot and Tikkun Olam

In addition to meditation and visualization practices, Kabbalistic healing also manifests through conscious action. The practice of Mitzvot (the commandments) is seen as a direct channel of healing, as each positive action brings a significant amount of spiritual light to the world.

For example:

Tzedakah (charity) is one of the most powerful Mitzvot for healing. By practicing acts of charity with pure intention, the practitioner activates the Sefirah of Chesed, bringing expansive healing to both themselves and the recipient. Tzedakah is especially effective in alleviating emotional suffering and restoring inner peace.

Shalom Bayit (peace in the home) is a practice that promotes harmony in family relationships and has a direct impact on emotional and mental health. Maintaining peace in the home activates the energies of Tiferet and Yesod, restoring balance between personal relationships and emotional stability.

Each Mitzvah, when performed with Kavanah (intention), not only aligns the individual with the divine will but also serves as a channel of spiritual, physical, and emotional healing.

Teshuvah (Repentance) and Healing

Teshuvah is another crucial aspect of Kabbalistic healing. Sincere repentance for mistakes made and a commitment to correcting those mistakes are seen as powerful means of clearing spiritual blockages and bringing renewal. In Kabbalah, sin is seen as an interruption in the flow of divine energies, and Teshuvah restores this flow.

Practice of Teshuvah for Healing: Take time to reflect on actions or behaviors that may have created spiritual blockages. Acknowledge these mistakes, ask for forgiveness, and commit to change. Visualize the white light of Binah (Understanding) flowing through you, purifying your spirit and opening the channels for divine energy to flow freely. This practice brings emotional and spiritual healing, restoring the integrity of the soul.

Kabbalistic healing is a profound process that involves restoring the balance between the Sefirot and aligning the body, mind, and spirit with the divine will. Through practices such as meditation, visualization, invocation of the Divine Names, Mitzvot, and Teshuvah, the practitioner can access the healing energies of the Sefirot and bring them into their daily life.

Chapter 13
Kabbalah and Psychology
The Integration of the Ego

The integration of the ego is a central theme in Kabbalah and, at the same time, an essential topic within modern psychology. Kabbalah teaches us that the ego, or the Yetzer Hara (evil inclination), is not simply a negative force to be eradicated, but rather a vital aspect of the human soul that needs to be understood and integrated in a balanced way. In the Kabbalistic tradition, the ego can be a powerful tool when aligned with the divine will, and its role is fundamental in our spiritual journey of Tikun (correction).

However, the ego can also be a significant obstacle to spiritual growth, especially when it manifests in an uncontrolled manner, leading to excessive pride, self-sufficiency, or separation from others. Thus, Kabbalah and modern psychology share the understanding that the ego should not be eliminated, but integrated and balanced with the higher spiritual purpose of the soul.

The Tree of Life, with its Sephirot, serves as a psychological and spiritual map that describes the process of ego integration. Each Sephirah can be seen as an aspect of the inner self that, when balanced, allows the ego to play its constructive role within the totality of the soul.

The Ego in Kabbalah and its Function

Within Kabbalah, the ego is closely related to the Sephirah of Malkhut, which represents the Kingdom, that is, the physical world and the way we manifest our individuality in the material world. Malkhut is the lowest Sephirah of the Tree of Life, and its role is to receive the energies of the other Sephirot and manifest them in the physical world. Thus, the ego plays a similar function: it is responsible for our earthly identity, our ability to act in the physical world, and to realize our spiritual potential.

However, Malkhut, when disconnected from the other Sephirot, can become egocentric and isolated. The ego, acting in isolation, can cause estrangement from the spiritual and divine purpose. On the other hand, when Malkhut is connected with the higher spheres, particularly with Tiferet (the central harmony of the Tree), the ego aligns with the higher will, serving as a channel for the manifestation of spiritual energies in the material world.

Therefore, the ego, in Kabbalah, is both a challenge and an essential tool. The key is to integrate it into our spiritual purpose, so that it serves as a means of expressing our true essence and contributing to the elevation of the soul and to Tikun Olam (the correction of the world).

The Psychology of the Ego: The Role of Yetzer Hara and Yetzer Hatov

Kabbalah teaches that human beings have two inclinations: the Yetzer Hara (evil inclination) and the Yetzer Hatov (good inclination). These two aspects are the forces that drive us to make decisions and act in the world. The Yetzer Hara is often associated with the ego, as it is responsible for our material desires, survival instincts, and self-preservation. The Yetzer Hatov, on the other hand, is related to our altruistic side, geared towards the common good and connection with the divine.

Modern psychology, especially in the field of psychoanalysis, echoes this duality through the concepts of id and superego, where the id represents primitive impulses and the superego represents moral norms and ideals. Between these two forces is the ego, which tries to balance instinctive desires with values and social expectations. Similarly, in Kabbalah, the ego (or the individual self) needs to balance the forces of Yetzer Hara and Yetzer Hatov, finding a path of harmony between our selfish desires and our spiritual responsibility.

Integration of the Ego and the Tree of Life

The Tree of Life is a powerful tool for understanding how the ego can be integrated and aligned with spiritual purpose. Each Sephirah offers a path to refine and balance the ego, allowing it to serve the development of the soul instead of blocking this process.

Keter (Crown) – Represents the highest level of the soul, the point of connection with the divine. In the integration of the ego, Keter teaches us to cultivate humility, recognizing that our individuality is only an expression of the divine will. When the ego is balanced with Keter, it becomes a vehicle for the manifestation of divine light in the world, instead of seeking personal glory.

Chochmah (Wisdom) and Binah (Understanding) – These two Sephirot offer a deeper understanding of the nature of the ego and how to integrate it. Chochmah connects us to spiritual intuition and higher wisdom, while Binah gives us the ability to reflect and understand our selfish impulses. Through these two Sephirot, we learn to discern when the ego is acting constructively or destructively.

Chesed (Kindness) and Gevurah (Strength) – The ego often manifests through expansive or restrictive behaviors. Chesed teaches us to cultivate altruism and generosity, while Gevurah teaches us to practice discipline and self-control. The ego balanced between these two forces expresses itself with kindness without indulgence and with discipline without excessive severity.

Tiferet (Beauty) – Tiferet is the central Sephirah that brings harmony to the ego. When the ego is aligned with Tiferet, it is able to express its individuality in a way that contributes to the well-being of the whole. Tiferet teaches us to balance our personal needs with service to others, reflecting the beauty of the soul through the balance between the Sephirot.

Netzach (Eternity) and Hod (Splendor) – These two Sephirot deal with the actions and reactions of the ego in the world. Netzach represents persistence and determination, while Hod reflects humility and acceptance. The healthy ego knows when to act with confidence and when to yield with humility, finding the balance between leadership and submission.

Yesod (Foundation) – Yesod is responsible for the integration of spiritual energies in the physical world. When the ego is aligned with Yesod, it allows spiritual light to flow through us in a balanced and constructive way. Yesod helps us maintain a healthy connection between body, mind, and spirit, facilitating the expression of divine purpose in the material world.

Malkhut (Kingdom) – Finally, Malkhut is where the ego fully manifests in the physical world. An ego aligned with Malkhut is able to realize its spiritual potential in a practical way, without getting lost in arrogance or selfishness. Malkhut teaches us to manifest our individuality in a way that benefits both ourselves and the world around us.

Techniques to Integrate the Ego

Kabbalah offers several practices to help integrate the ego in a constructive way. Some of these techniques are:

1. Meditation on the Sephirot:

Meditation on the Tree of Life allows the practitioner to visualize and integrate the different qualities of the Sephirot, balancing the ego with divine energies. By meditating on Tiferet, for example, the practitioner can cultivate inner balance, harmonizing the ego with spiritual and emotional well-being.

2. Daily reflection and self-assessment:

The practice of Hitbonenut (deep reflection) is essential to observe how the ego is influencing our actions. By taking a moment of the day to reflect on egocentric or altruistic behaviors, we can correct negative patterns and refine the ego in a constructive way.

3. Practice of Mitzvot (commandments):

The Mitzvot are channels of divine light that help align the ego with spiritual purpose. Fulfilling the Mitzvot with conscious intention is a way to discipline the ego, preventing it from dominating our actions and thoughts. The practice of Tzedakah (charity) is especially powerful, as it teaches the ego to let go of possessiveness and cultivate generosity.

4. Teshuvah (repentance):

The practice of Teshuvah helps us recognize when the ego is out of control and correct our mistakes. Teshuvah involves recognizing flaws, seeking reparation, and changing behavior. This allows the ego to realign with divine purpose, strengthening the process of Tikun (correction).

The integration of the ego is one of the most important challenges of the spiritual journey in Kabbalah. When the ego is balanced and aligned with the higher purpose of the soul, it becomes a tool for transformation and spiritual growth. The Tree of Life offers a detailed map for this integration, and Kabbalistic practices provide the means to achieve a harmonious balance between the inner self and the spiritual world.

Kabbalah, in its depth, offers mystical and spiritual tools that, when understood and applied, can transform the way we relate to the ego. Just as in modern psychology, where methods of self-assessment and self-reflection are essential for self-knowledge, Kabbalah encourages us to use meditative and reflective practices to achieve this state of internal balance.

Practices for Integrating the Ego with the Tree of Life

Meditation on the Sephirot is one of the most powerful practices for integrating the ego. Each Sephirah represents a divine quality that must be balanced in the life of the practitioner. Through meditation, the individual can harmonize these internal forces and learn to moderate the ego, aligning it with higher spiritual principles.

Meditation on the Sephirot

Keter (Crown): Meditating on Keter is meditating on the idea of maximum humility. The ego must be recognized as part of the whole, not as the center of everything. The practitioner focuses on their connection with the infinite, remembering that the ego is a vehicle to manifest the divine and not the ultimate goal. This meditation may involve repeating a mantra that refers to divine unity, such as "Ein Sof" (the Infinite).

Chochmah (Wisdom) and Binah (Understanding): These Sephirot work together, representing spiritual insight and intellectual analysis. During meditation, the practitioner reflects on how the ego responds to these qualities. Does the ego get lost in its own wisdom or seek to understand the divine with humility? Meditation on Chochmah and Binah invites the practitioner to discern between the intuitions that arise from the ego and those that come from the higher soul.

Chesed (Kindness) and Gevurah (Discipline): The balance between altruistic love (Chesed) and self-discipline (Gevurah) is crucial for the integration of the ego. Meditating on Chesed involves cultivating an attitude of generosity and kindness, realizing how the ego can serve others. On the other hand, meditating on Gevurah allows the practitioner to impose healthy limits on the ego, preventing excesses and destructive behaviors. Visualizing these two forces balancing in the soul is a fundamental practice for harmonizing the ego with the spirit.

Tiferet (Beauty): Tiferet, the center of the Tree of Life, represents harmony. When meditating on Tiferet, the practitioner seeks to balance all aspects of the soul, especially the ego, with spiritual purpose. Meditation here can involve visualizations of light, symbolizing the inner beauty and harmony of the being that reflects the divine. The ego must find its place within this beauty, not dominating, but serving the balance.

Netzach (Persistence) and Hod (Humility): These Sephirot are complementary. Meditation on Netzach invites the practitioner to reflect on their determination and how the ego deals with success and resistance. Meditation on Hod, on the other hand, cultivates humility and acceptance. The balanced ego knows when to insist and when to yield, when to take the lead and when to withdraw. Visualizing these two pillars working together is an essential exercise in moderating the ego.

Yesod (Foundation): Meditating on Yesod is meditating on the healthy expression of the ego in the physical world. The ego, when balanced, becomes a channel for divine energy. In this practice, the practitioner visualizes Yesod as a filter that purifies and balances the ego, allowing it to manifest spiritual purpose constructively.

Malkhut (Kingdom): Malkhut is the final manifestation, where the ego is fully expressed in the world. Meditating on Malkhut involves reflecting on how the ego acts in everyday interactions, especially in relation to power and control. Visualizing Malkhut as a kingdom that serves the greater good, rather than the whims of the ego, is a transformative practice.

Self-Assessment and Deep Reflection

The practice of Hitbonenut (self-reflection) is another powerful tool that Kabbalah offers us. During this process, the practitioner observes their daily thoughts, actions, and motivations, trying to identify when the ego is acting in an unbalanced way. Through self-assessment, it is possible to detect behavior patterns that indicate an inflated, self-centered ego or, conversely, a weakened and insecure ego.

Kabbalah teaches that a healthy ego is one that is aware of its limits and its spiritual function. It should not be suppressed, but refined. During the Hitbonenut exercise, it is helpful to ask yourself questions such as:

"Am I acting out of pride or for the love of the greater good?"

"Does my attitude today reflect the balance between Chesed and Gevurah?"

"Am I allowing my ego to serve the divine purpose?"

These daily reflections create a self-awareness that helps to moderate and transform the ego over time.

Teshuvah and the Cycle of Growth

Teshuvah (repentance or return) is an essential process for the integration of the ego. In Kabbalah, Teshuvah is seen as an opportunity not only to correct mistakes, but to transform the ego into a positive force. By recognizing mistakes and correcting egocentric behaviors, the practitioner begins to reconnect with the divine essence. Sincere repentance purifies the ego, allowing it to align more fully with the spiritual purpose of the soul.

The practice of Teshuvah involves recognition, reparation, and change. First, the practitioner recognizes where the ego has failed to serve the greater good. Then, they seek to repair the damage caused, whether emotional, spiritual, or physical. The process of Teshuvah is completed with the transformation of behavior, aligning the ego according to divine laws and Tikun (correction of the world).

Practical Exercises for Self-Balancing

To facilitate the integration of the ego, some simple practices can be incorporated into everyday life:

Practice of Tzedakah (Charity): Giving charity regularly, without seeking recognition, is a practical way to refine the ego. Tzedakah helps the practitioner to detach from selfishness and cultivate generosity.

Mantras and Affirmations: Using Kabbalistic mantras or daily affirmations that reinforce humility and service to the divine can help shape the ego's perspective. Phrases like "I serve the divine purpose" or "My true strength comes from the infinite light" can reprogram the mind for a healthy balance.

Journaling: Keeping a spiritual journal, in which the practitioner records their daily reflections, identifying moments of ego imbalance and ways to improve, is an excellent tool for self-development. This process allows the practitioner to track their progress in integrating the ego.

Kabbalah and Psychological Development

Modern psychology also offers valuable insights for the integration of the ego. Practices like cognitive-behavioral therapy (CBT) and mindfulness find parallels in Kabbalah. Just as Hitbonenut helps to reflect on the ego's behavior, CBT helps the practitioner identify destructive thought patterns and replace them with healthy ones.

Psychological development involves learning to coexist with the ego in a balanced way. Through Kabbalistic practices, it is possible to achieve a deeper understanding of the ego and its role in the spiritual journey, resulting in a more integrated mind and a higher spirit.

The integration of the ego, in the view of Kabbalah, is both a spiritual and psychological process. By balancing the forces of the Sephirot, reflecting on behavior, and practicing Teshuvah, the ego transforms into a powerful tool for the manifestation of divine light in the world. The practitioner, by engaging in these processes, not only becomes more aware of themselves, but also contributes to Tikun Olam, helping to repair the world around them.

Chapter 14
The Path of the Righteous Tzadik in Kabbalah

The concept of Tzadik, or "the righteous one," occupies a central role in Kabbalistic spirituality. In the Jewish tradition, a Tzadik is seen as an individual who has achieved a high level of righteousness, being someone who balances their personal desires with spiritual needs and acts constantly in alignment with divine commandments. The Tzadik, besides being a moral reference, is also a spiritual figure whose presence and actions help sustain and balance the world. According to Kabbalah, a Tzadik acts as a channel between the divine and the material world, positively influencing the cosmic balance. Kabbalah teaches us that we all have the potential to walk the path of the righteous, using spiritual tools and Kabbalistic practices to refine our thoughts, actions, and intentions. The path of the Tzadik is not reserved for a chosen few; it is a journey available to anyone who seeks righteousness and spiritual harmony.

The Mission of the Tzadik in Kabbalah

In Kabbalah, the concept of Tikkun Olam (correction of the world) is closely related to the role of the Tzadik. The Tzadik acts as an agent of healing and repair, helping to bring harmony between the spiritual and material worlds. His mission is not only his own spiritual elevation but also to contribute to the balance and rectification of the world as a whole. The Tzadik is seen as someone who reflects divine light in the world, living according to the teachings of the Sephirot and incorporating the harmony of the Tree of Life in his daily life. His presence acts as a pillar of stability in the cosmos, helping to maintain the balance between the forces of chaos and order. In Kabbalistic literature, there is a common expression: "The world is sustained thanks to the righteous." This means that the righteousness and good deeds of people like the Tzadik have a profound and positive impact on the cosmic order.

The Qualities of a Tzadik

The path of the Tzadik is marked by various qualities and virtues that Kabbalah values. Among them are:

Humility: The Tzadik recognizes that his strength and wisdom come from a higher source. His humility is one of the most important qualities, as it allows him to serve as a pure channel for divine energy. Humility, in Kabbalah, is associated with the Sephirah of Keter, the crown that represents the supreme principle of surrender to the divine.

Altruism: The Tzadik acts for the benefit of others. He puts the needs of the community and the world ahead of his personal desires. This is deeply linked to the Sephirah of Chesed (kindness), which expresses the ability to give without expecting anything in return.

Discipline: Although the Tzadik is compassionate and kind, he also knows when to exercise restraint and discipline. This quality is related to the Sephirah of Gevurah (strength), which balances Chesed. A Tzadik knows when to impose limits and how to guide others firmly, without losing his loving essence.

Harmony: The Tzadik is able to find balance between the opposing forces of life. He is the living example of the Sephirah of Tiferet (beauty), which represents the harmony between kindness and severity. His life is a reflection of this spiritual beauty, which manifests in the form of harmony between body, mind, and spirit.

Persistence: The Tzadik demonstrates perseverance in his spiritual journey. He knows that the path of righteousness is full of challenges but maintains his faith and dedication, overcoming obstacles with determination. This quality aligns with the Sephirah of Netzach (eternity), which represents the ability to continue, regardless of difficulties.

Reflective Humility: Related to the Sephirah of Hod (splendor), this quality reflects the Tzadik's ability to be introspective, always seeking ways to improve his service to the divine. He is constantly reflecting on his actions, learning from his mistakes, and growing spiritually.

Foundation: The Sephirah of Yesod (foundation) is linked to the Tzadik's ability to be a channel for the divine, keeping his life grounded in spirituality and his connections to the world. The Tzadik is like a bridge between heaven and earth, channeling higher energies to the material world.

Royalty and Service: Finally, the Tzadik acts in the world of Malchut (kingdom), the sphere where spirituality fully manifests in the physical world. Although he lives among others, he serves as an example of spiritual leadership and service, guiding others toward spiritual growth.

The Tzadik as a Channel of Light

One of the most striking characteristics of a Tzadik is his ability to serve as a channel of light. In Kabbalah, this means that he opens himself to divine spiritual energies and reflects them into the physical world, helping to elevate and transform those around him. This ability is especially important in the context of Tikkun Olam, as the Tzadik is a stabilizing force, working to heal the world from the spiritual ruptures that arise from the disconnection between man and the divine. The Tzadik does not see separation between the spiritual and the physical. Instead, he recognizes that the material world is only an extension of the spiritual, and his actions aim to unite these two realities. He constantly works to purify his intentions and align them with the divine purpose, serving as an example for others and, often, inspiring them to follow a similar path.

Examples of Tzadikim in the Kabbalistic Tradition

Throughout history, many individuals have been recognized as Tzadikim. They range from great spiritual masters to ordinary people who, through their righteous and compassionate actions, brought light and healing to the world.

Rabbi Shimon bar Yochai: Considered the author of the Zohar, the central text of Kabbalah, Rabbi Shimon is one of the most revered examples of a Tzadik. He spent much of his life teaching the esoteric secrets of the Torah and helping his students achieve higher spiritual levels.

Baal Shem Tov: Founder of the Hasidic movement, the Baal Shem Tov is another example of a Tzadik who inspired millions with his teachings on joy, faith, and service to God. He believed that even the humblest people could achieve high levels of righteousness through sincere devotion.

Rabbi Yitzchak Luria (the Ari): Known as the Ari, he is one of the greatest masters of Kabbalah. His teachings on the repair of the world and the role of the Tzadik as a cosmic force of balance are followed to this day.

These Tzadikim were not only spiritual sages but also community leaders, known for their kindness, compassion, and willingness to help others. They lived their lives in service to others, demonstrating that the path of righteousness is accessible to all.

The Call to Be a Tzadik

Kabbalah teaches that every human being has the potential to become a Tzadik. This does not mean that everyone will be perfect, but that each person can constantly work to refine their character, align their actions with the divine, and serve the greater good. The process of becoming a Tzadik involves:

Constant self-assessment: Reflecting on one's thoughts and actions, always seeking to improve.

Development of virtues: Practicing kindness, humility, and discipline.

Alignment with the divine: Seeking a deep spiritual connection through prayer, meditation, and study.

Service to others: Putting the needs of the community and the world above one's own.

This is a journey that requires dedication and persistence, but the reward is a life of inner peace, purpose, and connection with the divine. The path of the Tzadik in Kabbalah is a powerful model of spiritual life. It teaches us that true righteousness is not found only in external actions but in an internal balance that reflects the divine qualities of kindness, humility, discipline, and service. We are all called to follow this path, seeking our own transformation and contributing to the elevation of the world around us.

The Daily Spiritual Practice of the Tzadik

Although the Tzadik is an elevated figure, his life is marked by daily practices that anyone can adopt. The difference lies in the intention and dedication with which these practices are carried out. For a Tzadik, every action, no matter how simple, is permeated by the intention to serve the divine and the greater good. The focus is not only on great works but on attention to the details of everyday life, such as interactions with others, prayers, and meditation practices.

1. Prayer as a Constant Connection

Prayer is one of the main tools of the Tzadik to stay connected with the divine. According to Kabbalah, prayer is not just a recitation of words but an act of deep communication with God. The Tzadik sees prayer as an opportunity to align with spiritual forces and attract blessings to the world. His prayer is made with humility and pure intention, reflecting his desire to be a channel for divine light. An example is the practice of Kavanah, conscious intention during prayer. The Tzadik seeks to put all his heart and soul into each recited word, transforming prayer into an experience of unity with the divine. Kavanah allows the Tzadik to elevate himself spiritually and bring healing and harmony to the world. For practitioners who aspire to walk the path of the Tzadik, daily prayer with Kavanah is an essential tool. Kabbalah suggests the use of Psalms and other sacred texts as a way to connect to higher spiritual energies, promoting peace and righteousness both for oneself and for the surrounding community.

2. Practice of Chesed (Kindness and Altruism)

Chesed (love and kindness) is one of the fundamental qualities of a Tzadik, and this practice goes beyond sporadic gestures of charity. The Tzadik practices Chesed daily, seeking ways to help others in all aspects of his life, whether offering emotional, material, or spiritual support. He sees each interaction as an opportunity to spread kindness and uplift those around him. To adopt this practice, it is necessary to develop awareness of the needs of others and have an active approach to helping without expecting anything in return. This can be done through simple actions, such as listening to someone attentively, offering words of encouragement, or performing acts of Tzedakah (charity), whether with material donations or offering time and energy in service to others. The practice of Chesed is considered a spiritual pillar because, according to Kabbalah, active kindness has the power to open spiritual portals and attract blessings. When the individual acts with genuine altruism, he is reflecting the light of the Sephirah of Chesed, channeling the divine energy of love into the physical world.

3. Gevurah: The Discipline of the Righteous

Although kindness is essential, the Tzadik also knows how to balance it with Gevurah, the strength of discipline and restraint. This Sephirah teaches that discipline is necessary to maintain harmony. The Tzadik applies Gevurah by moderating his desires, maintaining control over his impulses, and ensuring that his actions are guided by wisdom and the need of the moment, rather than by the whims of the ego. The practice of Gevurah involves establishing healthy boundaries, both for oneself and for others, without losing compassion. For those who wish to follow the path of the Tzadik, constant self-assessment is fundamental. This includes reflecting on the intentions behind each action and maintaining a disciplined posture that balances generosity with the need to protect one's own energy and resources. A practical way to apply Gevurah is to create daily moments of silence and reflection, in which the practitioner reviews his actions and motivations, ensuring that they are in harmony with spiritual principles. The Tzadik does this constantly, purifying his intentions and ensuring that his discipline is in service to the divine.

4. Tiferet: The Harmony of the Heart

Tiferet, which represents beauty and harmony, is the central essence of the Tzadik. Tiferet reflects the perfect balance between the forces of Chesed and Gevurah, and the Tzadik expresses this harmony in all areas of his life. He is neither excessively indulgent nor too rigid; instead, he seeks to integrate polarities to create a life marked by beauty and justice. The Tzadik practices Tiferet by living in a way that his actions and behaviors reflect divine beauty. This means acting in a balanced and just manner, both with oneself and with others. Those who aspire to walk the path of the Tzadik can cultivate Tiferet by seeking to live a life of integrity and emotional balance, treating others with justice but also with compassion. The practice of Tiferet can be developed through daily meditations that focus on inner harmony. Visualizing the Tree of Life and the centrality of Tiferet helps the practitioner integrate this quality, bringing emotional balance and clarity in decisions.

Spiritual Discipline: Paths to Righteousness

Spiritual discipline is essential on the path of the Tzadik. Kabbalah teaches us that to live a life of righteousness, it is necessary to have self-control, dedication, and a strong sense of spiritual purpose. The Tzadik not only acts in a righteous manner but also lives in a constant state of spiritual growth and refinement.

1. Hitbodedut: Meditation of Isolation

A powerful practice that the Tzadik adopts is Hitbodedut, a form of solitary meditation in which the practitioner withdraws to be alone with his thoughts and prayers. This moment of inner connection is an opportunity for the Tzadik to reflect on his life, his actions, and his relationship with the divine. Hitbodedut allows the practitioner to create an intimate relationship with God, openly discussing his difficulties and expressing gratitude. In the practice of Hitbodedut, the practitioner can meditate on the Sephirot, reflecting on how these divine forces are present in his life and how he can better align himself with them. This daily meditation is an anchor point for the Tzadik, helping him maintain his clear spiritual perception and his commitment to the path of justice.

2. Study of the Torah and the Zohar

The Tzadik dedicates himself to the study of the Torah, especially the passages that reveal the mysteries of spirituality, such as the Zohar. Kabbalah teaches that the study of the Torah is a way to connect directly with divine wisdom, and the Tzadik delves deeply into this study to understand how to apply these teachings in practical life. Those who wish to follow this path can integrate the study of the Torah and Kabbalah into their daily routines, seeking to learn not only the esoteric aspects but also how these teachings manifest in everyday life. The Zohar, for example, offers profound insights into the nature of the soul, the spiritual forces that shape the universe, and the role of the Tzadik as a channel of light.

Becoming a Tzadik in Action

The path of the Tzadik is not just theoretical; it is a continuous practice that manifests in everyday actions.

Those who aspire to approach this righteousness should seek to live according to the following principles:

Serve others: The Tzadik puts the needs of the community first. Engaging in charity work, emotional support, or spiritual guidance are practical ways to apply this principle.

Constant spiritual refinement: The Tzadik is always seeking ways to purify his thoughts and actions, aligning himself with the divine will.

Develop Kavanah: Every action is done with intention and focus, from prayer to daily acts of kindness.

The journey to becoming a Tzadik is one of the most profound expressions of Kabbalistic spirituality. It is a path of self-transformation, service to others, and connection with the divine. Through daily spiritual practices, such as prayer with Kavanah, meditation, and the study of the Torah, anyone can begin to walk this path of righteousness and spiritual elevation. By living with humility, kindness, and discipline, the practitioner not only elevates his own soul but also contributes to the balance and healing of the world.

Chapter 15
The Hidden Wisdom of the Psalms

The Psalms occupy a prominent place within the Kabbalistic tradition. These poems and prayers, mostly composed by King David, are seen in Kabbalah as portals to access deep spiritual dimensions. Through the recitation and meditation on the Psalms, the practitioner is able to connect with the divine forces that shape the universe and influence their daily life. In Kabbalah, it is believed that every word, every phrase, and every intonation of the Psalms contains a hidden spiritual meaning, capable of healing, protecting, and elevating the soul. Since ancient times, the Psalms have been used both as a source of spiritual comfort and as an instrument of mystical power. They are recited in moments of anguish, danger, gratitude, praise, and celebration. In the Kabbalistic view, the Psalms are not only expressions of faith but spiritual tools that, when used correctly, have the potential to activate divine energies and transform realities.

The Mystical Power of the Psalms

Kabbalists believe that the Psalms possess a hidden power, a spiritual energy that can be released when recited with the correct intention. In Kabbalistic practice, *Kavanah* (spiritual intention) is fundamental to unlocking the power contained in the words of the Psalms. This means that mechanical or inattentive recitation will not have the same effect as a recitation with focus and devotion. To access the mystical wisdom of the Psalms, it is essential to meditate deeply on their meaning and pronounce them with heart and soul.

According to the Zohar, the central book of Kabbalah, the Psalms contain keys to accessing different levels of consciousness and spiritual worlds. They were written in a language that goes beyond literal understanding, using metaphors, symbols, and images that reflect deeper spiritual truths. Each Psalm can be understood on multiple levels, from the simplest to the most esoteric.

Kabbalists also associate the Psalms with certain *Sefirot* of the Tree of Life. For example, Psalms that speak of mercy are linked to the *Sefirah* of *Chesed*, while those that deal with justice are associated with *Gevurah*. By reciting a Psalm with the appropriate *Kavanah*, the practitioner can channel the energies of these *Sefirot*, using them to achieve healing, protection, or spiritual elevation.

The Structure of the Psalms and Their Hidden Meaning

The 150 Psalms that make up the Book of Psalms are divided into five smaller books, which, according to Kabbalists, corresponds to the five books of the Torah. Just as the Torah reveals the mysteries of creation, divine revelation, and the spiritual journey of humanity, the Psalms function as a bridge that connects the practitioner to the divine universe, allowing them to navigate between the spiritual and material dimensions.

Each Psalm is seen as a spiritual vibration, and the sound of its words, when recited correctly, creates waves of energy that reverberate in the spiritual world. Therefore, Kabbalists emphasize the importance of learning the correct intonation and pronunciation of the Hebrew words of the Psalms, so that the mystical energy contained in them is fully activated.

Some of the Psalms are considered particularly powerful within Kabbalah. For example:

Psalm 23 ("The Lord is my shepherd; I shall not want") is often recited to invoke spiritual protection and confidence in difficult circumstances.

Psalm 91 is known for its ability to protect against negative forces and unseen dangers.

Psalm 121 ("I lift up my eyes to the hills") is recited to ask for divine help in moments of doubt and uncertainty.

The Kabbalistic Interpretation of the Psalms

Kabbalah teaches that the Psalms were inspired directly by God, and each word contains hidden secrets that can only be understood through deep study and meditation. Many Kabbalists use the system of *Gematria*, which assigns numerical values to Hebrew letters, to reveal the mystical connections hidden in the words of the Psalms.

For example, the Tetragrammaton (YHVH), the most sacred name of God, appears frequently in the Psalms. When recited with the appropriate *Kavanah*, it invokes the creative energy and protective force of the divine. The combination of letters, sounds, and intentions creates an energy field that can directly influence the physical and spiritual reality of the practitioner.

Furthermore, Kabbalists teach that the Psalms can be used as a means of accessing higher worlds. Each Psalm corresponds to a specific level of existence, and its recitation opens portals that allow the practitioner to connect with these dimensions. This is particularly important in meditative practices, where the practitioner focuses on a specific Psalm to travel through the worlds of Kabbalah (*Assiyah*, *Yetzirah*, *Beriah*, and *Atzilut*) and obtain visions or spiritual guidance.

Psalms and Spiritual Protection

In Kabbalah, the Psalms are often used as spiritual amulets for protection against negative forces, illnesses, and even enemies. Many Kabbalists carry scrolls with written Psalms, believing that these texts have the power to repel negative influences and attract blessings.

The tradition suggests that the Psalms should not be used merely as magic words, but with the clear intention of aligning with the divine will and attracting light and harmony into the practitioner's life. For example, reciting Psalm 91 when facing dangerous situations is a common practice among those who follow Kabbalah, as this Psalm is known for its power of spiritual protection.

The Psalms are also used in spiritual healing rituals. When recited over a sick person, with the proper *Kavanah*, the Psalms can attract healing forces and accelerate the recovery process. The healing power of the Psalms is reinforced by the fact that they invoke the name of God and channel energies from the *Sefirot* to restore the spiritual balance of the body.

The Practice of Meditating on the Psalms

Besides being recited, the Psalms can also be used as a focus for deep meditation. In Kabbalistic meditation, the practitioner focuses on the words and letters of the Psalms, allowing their esoteric meaning to be revealed on deeper levels of consciousness.

A common practice is to choose a specific Psalm that is related to a spiritual question or goal and recite it repeatedly, allowing the mind to calm down and the hidden wisdom of the text to emerge. During this meditation, the practitioner may visualize the Hebrew letters floating before their eyes or forming patterns of light, connecting with the spiritual energies associated with those letters.

For example, when meditating on Psalm 23, the practitioner may visualize the "divine shepherd" as a protective light that guides them through difficulties and obstacles, feeling enveloped by the comforting presence of God. The practice of meditation on the Psalms allows the individual to align with the spiritual energies that the texts invoke, creating a deep connection between the body, mind, and spirit.

The Mystical Language of the Psalms

The language of the Psalms is rich in poetic images and mystical symbols that reveal spiritual truths about the universe and the relationship of human beings with the divine. Kabbalists believe that each image— whether the "shepherd" of Psalm 23 or the "hills" of

Psalm 121—is a representation of spiritual forces in action.

For example, when King David speaks of the "rod and staff" that comfort him, he is symbolically referring to the forces of *Chesed* (kindness) and *Gevurah* (discipline), which together bring balance to the soul. Similarly, the "overflowing cup" is a reference to the spiritual abundance that flows when the practitioner aligns with the divine will.

Kabbalists study the Psalms deeply to discover the symbolic layers contained in each verse. With practice, the reader begins to realize that the words go beyond their literal meaning and serve as keys to open spiritual portals.

The Psalms, as taught in Kabbalah, are much more than simple prayers; they are mystical tools that, when used with the correct intention, have the power to transform lives, heal spiritual wounds, and offer protection against negative forces. By delving into the hidden wisdom of the Psalms, the practitioner begins to unravel the deep mysteries of Kabbalistic spirituality and access a higher dimension of existence.

In the second part of this study on the Psalms, we will explore specific Kabbalistic practices that allow the practitioner to use the Psalms for healing, protection, and spiritual elevation, and how to integrate them into daily life as part of a continuous path of spiritual transformation.

The Kabbalistic practice with the Psalms goes beyond reading and meditation. In Kabbalah, the Psalms are used as powerful instruments of spiritual transformation, which allow the practitioner to achieve healing, protection, and elevation.

The Practical Use of the Psalms for Healing

In the Kabbalistic tradition, the Psalms have been widely used for spiritual and physical healing. The ancient Kabbalists saw the words of the Psalms as vehicles of divine energy, capable of restoring the balance between the body and the soul. The belief is that illness is not only a physical condition but also a reflection of a spiritual imbalance, and, therefore, the Psalms have the power to heal by realigning the person's spiritual energies.

1. Choosing the Right Psalm for Healing

Each Psalm has a specific purpose within the Kabbalistic tradition, and the healing Psalms are selected according to the nature of the affliction. Some of the most used include:

Psalm 6: This Psalm is recited to ask for healing in situations of serious physical illness. It calls for divine compassion and the restoration of health, recognizing human frailty in the face of adversity.

Psalm 30: Recited to overcome sadness and depression, this Psalm is a prayer for light to return after periods of emotional or spiritual darkness.

Psalm 41: Used to ask for physical and emotional healing, especially in cases where the person is dealing with prolonged health problems or mental imbalances.

The practice consists of reciting the chosen Psalm with concentrated intention (*Kavanah*), visualizing the body and soul being filled with divine healing light. The recitation can be done several times a day, until the practitioner feels a change in energy or a relief from the symptoms.

2. Recitation Technique for Healing

Slow and focused recitation is essential to release the mystical power of the Psalms. When chanting the words, the practitioner should focus on the Hebrew letters, visualizing them as rays of light that enter the body, restoring and healing. The Hebrew letters are seen as channels of divine energy, and each sound they produce reverberates in the spiritual plane.

In addition, the practitioner can use the visualization of the *Sefirot* during the recitation. For example, when reciting Psalm 6, the practitioner can visualize the healing light of *Chesed* flowing through their body, bringing compassion and balance. For situations that involve strength or resistance, the light of *Gevurah* can be visualized as a protective and stabilizing force.

The practice should be accompanied by deep and conscious breaths, allowing the body to relax and be receptive to the spiritual energy that is being invoked. When combined with the recitation, this state of calm allows the healing energies to flow freely, promoting the restoration of health.

Spiritual Protection with the Psalms

Kabbalah teaches that, in addition to promoting healing, the Psalms can be used for spiritual protection against negative forces and evil influences. Kabbalists believe that the words of the Psalms create an energetic shield around the practitioner, warding off evil and bringing spiritual security.

1. Psalms of Protection Against Negative Forces

The Psalms are often recited to protect against physical dangers, but also against adverse spiritual influences. Some of the best-known Psalms for protection include:

Psalm 91: Perhaps the most famous of the Psalms of protection, this text is recited to ward off visible and invisible dangers, including physical enemies, illnesses, and spiritual attacks. It is considered a true spiritual shield.

Psalm 121: Recited when the person is facing challenges and uncertainties, this Psalm asks for direct protection from God, invoking the constant guard of the Creator.

Psalm 27: Used in times of fear or oppression, this Psalm strengthens trust in the divine as protector and ensures the overcoming of any evil.

These Psalms should be recited daily, especially in situations of vulnerability or when the practitioner feels that they are being influenced by negative external forces. In Kabbalistic practice, it is believed that the regular recitation of Psalms of protection creates a field of energy that wards off evil and harmonizes the environment.

2. Creating Spiritual Amulets with the Psalms

Kabbalists also teach that the Psalms can be written on scrolls and carried as amulets of protection. These scrolls, known as *Kameot*, are traditionally handwritten by a trained scribe and imbued with spiritual intentions during the writing process. The practitioner can carry the *Kamea* with them for constant protection.

Although this type of amulet is powerful, the focus should always be on spiritual intention. The Psalms should not be seen as magic words that work on their own, but as channels of divine energy, activated by faith and intention. When carrying a *Kamea*, the practitioner should keep their mind and heart tuned to the divine light, remembering that true protection comes from their spiritual connection with God.

Spiritual Elevation Through the Psalms

The recitation of the Psalms is not only a practice of healing and protection but also a tool for elevating the soul. In Kabbalah, the human soul is seen as a divine spark, which constantly seeks to return to its spiritual source. The Psalms are seen as spiritual bridges that allow the practitioner to ascend to higher levels of consciousness and connection with the divine.

1. Psalms for Spiritual Purification

Many Psalms are used to purify the soul of negative energies and to free oneself from destructive emotions, such as anger, fear, and sadness. Some of the most recommended Psalms for purification include:

Psalm 51: This Psalm is a prayer of repentance and spiritual purification, asking God to cleanse the heart and soul of all impurities. It is often recited in times of repentance or when the practitioner seeks spiritual reconciliation.

Psalm 32: A Psalm that promotes emotional healing and spiritual elevation, helping to alleviate the burden of guilt and open the heart to forgiveness.

The practice of spiritual purification involves deep meditation on the words of the Psalm, allowing them to cleanse the negative emotions and energies that may be blocking the spiritual path. When reciting these Psalms, the practitioner visualizes the divine light purifying their heart and mind, releasing all the weight that hinders spiritual progress.

2. Psalms for Elevation and Union with the Divine

Through the Psalms, Kabbalists seek not only protection and healing but also mystical union with the Creator. Some Psalms are recited with the intention of elevating the soul to the highest levels of consciousness, providing a direct experience of the presence of God. Psalm 63, for example, is a song of longing for divine proximity, expressing the soul's desire to be in union with the Creator.

By meditating on these Psalms, the practitioner can achieve elevated states of mystical contemplation, where the boundaries between the physical and spiritual world dissolve. The soul, through the sacred words, is guided back to its divine origin, connecting to the energies of the *Sefirot* and experiencing the direct presence of God. Practices of Intonation and Singing of the Psalms

In Kabbalah, the Psalms can also be recited through singing and melodic intonation, a practice that increases their spiritual power. The tradition of singing the Psalms dates back to the time of the Temple in Jerusalem, where they were sung as part of spiritual rituals. Today, this practice continues as a way to amplify the spiritual vibrations of the Psalms.

Singing the Psalms with specific melodies creates a profound effect on both the body and the soul. The melodies help to harmonize emotions and create an energetic field conducive to meditation and spiritual elevation. Many Kabbalists believe that the sound of the sung words directly reaches the spiritual spheres, accelerating the process of healing, protection, or ascension.

The practitioner can create their own intuitive melody when reciting the Psalms or use traditional melodies, which have been passed down from generation to generation. The important thing is that the intonation be done with devotion and clear intention, allowing the words to resonate deeply within oneself.
Integration of the Psalms in Daily Life

For the practitioner of Kabbalah, the Psalms can be integrated into daily life as part of a continuous spiritual practice. The daily recitation of Psalms not only strengthens the connection with the divine but also brings harmony and balance to the practitioner's life.

It is recommended to start the day with the recitation of a Psalm that inspires gratitude and protection, such as Psalm 100 or Psalm 121, and end the day with a Psalm of purification and reflection, such as Psalm 4. In this way, the Psalms can be used to mark sacred rhythms throughout the day, bringing the sacred into every moment of life.

The Kabbalistic practice with the Psalms is rich and multifaceted, offering tools for healing, protection, and spiritual elevation. By delving into this practice, the practitioner discovers that the Psalms are not only ancient texts but living channels of spiritual energy, capable of profoundly transforming their life. Whether through recitation, meditation, or singing, the Psalms continue to be a powerful bridge between the physical and spiritual worlds.

Chapter 16
Kabbalah and the Cycle of Jewish Holidays

The Jewish holidays, more than simple religious celebrations, are, in the Kabbalistic tradition, powerful spiritual portals. Each of these festivities is associated with specific energies that offer the practitioner the opportunity to achieve spiritual elevation, purification, and transformation. In Kabbalah, time is not seen as a straight line, but as a dynamic cycle, where certain moments of the year allow access to unique spiritual forces, linked to the divine energies in constant flux.

Throughout the cycle of Jewish holidays, these energies allow the practitioner, when aware of their potential, to use each occasion to work on deep aspects of their soul and their connection with the divine.

The Jewish Calendar and Cyclical Time in Kabbalah

The Jewish calendar, as well as the annual cycle of holidays, is deeply intertwined with Kabbalistic teachings. Unlike the Gregorian calendar, which follows a solar pattern, the Jewish calendar is lunisolar, meaning it combines lunar cycles with the correction of the solar cycle. This balance between the sun and the moon represents in Kabbalah the harmony between masculine and feminine forces, which manifest in nature and in human souls.

Each Jewish holiday is like an anchor point that allows the practitioner to synchronize with the spiritual energy of that moment. By celebrating these holidays with full awareness of their mystical meaning, the practitioner tunes into the energy flows that influence both the universe and the soul itself.

Rosh Hashanah: The New Year and Divine Judgment

Rosh Hashanah, the Jewish New Year, marks the beginning of a new spiritual cycle. In Kabbalah, this is the moment when all of creation undergoes divine judgment. God, in this period, evaluates each soul, each being, determining the destiny of all for the following year. However, this judgment is not just an immutable decree. Kabbalists teach that, through spiritual reflection and sincere repentance, it is possible to positively influence the decrees that will be written in the Book of Life.

The energy of Rosh Hashanah is associated with the Sefirah of Malkhut, which represents divine reign over the physical world. During this period, the practitioner is invited to recognize God's sovereignty, reflect on their past actions, and make a spiritual commitment to the new cycle that is beginning.

Kabbalistic practice during this period involves meditation on the Divine Names related to creation and judgment, especially the Tetragrammaton (YHVH), and the recitation of prayers that open the heart to the process of divine judgment. The central idea is to align with the divine will so that the next year is full of spiritual growth and achievements.

Yom Kippur: The Day of Atonement and the Purification of the Soul

Ten days after Rosh Hashanah comes Yom Kippur, the Day of Atonement, the most sacred moment of the Jewish calendar. Yom Kippur is the culmination of the process of repentance initiated on Rosh Hashanah. In Kabbalah, this is the moment of maximum purification of the soul, when the spiritual barriers between human beings and God are removed. It is a period in which the soul can return to its purest state, like a clean vessel ready to receive divine light.

The energy of Yom Kippur is strongly linked to the Sefirah of Gevurah, which represents rigor and discipline. However, this rigor is used in a positive way, as a force of transformation and rectification. The fasting and restrictions observed on this day are intended to purify the body and mind, removing material distractions so that the practitioner can focus on the spiritual essence.

During Yom Kippur, Kabbalists meditate deeply on the *Tikkun* (correction) of spiritual and emotional flaws. Practices such as confession and asking for forgiveness are central, and they should be accompanied by a genuine intention not to repeat past mistakes. At the end of Yom Kippur, the soul is prepared to receive a new influx of spiritual light, being closer to its divine essence.

Sukkot: The Feast of Tabernacles and the Joy of Connection with the Divine

Soon after Yom Kippur, Sukkot, the Feast of Tabernacles, begins. This holiday celebrates the divine protection that the Israelites received during their journey through the desert, living in temporary shelters. In Kabbalah, Sukkot is a celebration of spiritual joy, representing a moment when the soul can feel completely protected by the divine presence.

The temporary hut, known as a Sukkah, represents the fragile material shell of human existence, while the presence of God symbolizes the spiritual light that protects and sustains the practitioner. Sukkot is associated with the Sefirah of Chesed, the divine emanation of kindness, and during this period, the emphasis is on recognizing and celebrating the divine abundance that flows into the world.

Kabbalistic practices during Sukkot include meditation in the Sukkah as a symbol of spiritual protection and the elevation of consciousness beyond material concerns. Another important symbol of Sukkot is the Lulav and Etrog (a palm branch and a citrus fruit), which represent the unification of the different forces of creation. By shaking the Lulav and Etrog in different directions, the practitioner symbolizes the harmonization of divine energies in all corners of the universe.

Passover: The Feast of Liberation and the Purification from Spiritual Slavery

Passover, the Jewish Passover, commemorates the liberation of the Israelites from slavery in Egypt. In Kabbalah, Passover is not just a celebration of physical freedom, but a spiritual liberation. Each person, on some level, is enslaved to negative patterns, whether they are emotional, psychological, or spiritual. Passover offers the practitioner the opportunity to break free from these bonds and begin a new cycle of growth and ascension.

Passover is associated with the Sefirah of Tiferet, which represents harmony and compassion. During this holiday, the focus is on the purification of the soul. The *Chametz* (leavened bread), which is removed from all homes during Passover, symbolizes the inflated ego and the temptations that prevent us from reaching our spiritual potential. By removing the *Chametz*, the practitioner symbolically purifies themselves of these negative influences.

The Seder night, the ritual meal that begins Passover, is one of the most spiritually charged moments of the year. Every detail of the Seder is full of Kabbalistic symbolism, from the four cups of wine that represent the four divine emanations, to the narrative of the Exodus, which is a metaphor for the soul's journey towards spiritual freedom.

Shavuot: The Revelation and the Connection with Divine Wisdom

Shavuot is the holiday that commemorates the giving of the Torah at Mount Sinai. In the Kabbalistic tradition, Shavuot represents the moment of direct connection with divine wisdom. This is the period in which the soul can open itself to receive new levels of spiritual understanding.

The energy of Shavuot is connected to the Sefirah of Binah, which is the emanation of deep understanding. During Shavuot, the practitioner seeks to expand their spiritual consciousness, meditating on the divine teachings and integrating them into their life.

Kabbalistic practice during Shavuot involves meditation on the giving of the Torah and reflection on how spiritual wisdom can be used to transform everyday life. Many practitioners spend the night of Shavuot studying sacred texts, in an effort to capture the divine light that is especially accessible during this period.

The cycle of Jewish holidays, in light of Kabbalah, offers a series of opportunities for the practitioner to connect with the spiritual forces that flow through the universe. Each holiday brings a unique energy, which can be harnessed for purification, elevation, and spiritual transformation. By aligning with these energies, the practitioner tunes into the divine cycle, living in a more harmonious and conscious way.

The Jewish holidays are not mere commemorative dates, but spiritual portals that, according to Kabbalah, offer opportunities for personal elevation and transformation. Each one carries a unique energy, linked to the Sefirot and the annual cycle of spiritual life. In this part, the focus will be on the Kabbalistic practices and rituals associated with these festivities, allowing the reader to align their actions with the spiritual purpose of each one. In addition to providing celebration and renewal, these rituals help to access and channel the divine energies available in each sacred period.

Practices of Rosh Hashanah: Judgment and Renewal

Rosh Hashanah, the Jewish New Year, is a time of deep introspection and spiritual alignment. The first step for the practitioner, according to Kabbalah, is the conscious preparation for the divine judgment that occurs during these two days. The blowing of the Shofar is a central ritual. The Shofar, a ram's horn, is not just a sound instrument; its sound, in the Kabbalistic view, awakens the soul and removes the spiritual barriers that have formed during the year.

Before Rosh Hashanah, many Kabbalists practice *Tashlich*, a ritual in which they go to a body of water, symbolizing the desire to cast the sins and negativities of the previous year to the bottom of the waters. This act represents the willingness to break free from spiritual impurities and make room for new light.

On a meditative level, Kabbalists reflect deeply on the Sefirah of Malkhut, the divine emanation related to reign and realization. The question that is asked during these meditations is: "How can I align myself more with the divine plan?". This focus helps the practitioner create intentions for the next cycle and open themselves to the spiritual blessings of Rosh Hashanah.

The Day of Yom Kippur: Spiritual Cleansing

After the initial process of judgment on Rosh Hashanah, Yom Kippur emerges as the Day of Atonement, the culmination of repentance and purification. The complete fast and the restriction of material pleasures are practices that, according to Kabbalah, allow the practitioner to transcend the physical body and focus entirely on the soul. It is said that on Yom Kippur, the soul reaches the state closest to its divine essence, free from the distractions of the physical world.

One of the most important rituals is the *Viddui*, the confession of sins, which is repeated multiple times during the day. Confession is not seen only as an acknowledgment of the mistakes made, but as an act of self-transformation. By confessing, the practitioner not only repents but also declares the intention to correct the spiritual imbalances.

Meditation on Yom Kippur revolves around the Sefirah of Gevurah, which represents rigor and judgment. Here, the practitioner seeks to balance this energy with the force of Chesed (kindness), understanding that severe judgment exists to facilitate healing and renewal. At the end of Yom Kippur, the practitioner is spiritually renewed, ready for a new cycle of life and growth.

Sukkot: The Encounter with the Divine in the Sukkah

Soon after Yom Kippur, the celebration of Sukkot, the Feast of Tabernacles, begins, which symbolizes the divine protection received by the Israelites during their journey in the desert. The practitioner builds and temporarily inhabits a Sukkah (hut), which represents the transitory nature of material life and the need to trust in divine protection.

In Kabbalah, the Sukkah is also seen as a microcosm of the Sefirah of Chesed, a sacred space where the energy of love and divine protection permeates the environment. Entering the Sukkah is an act of trusting in God's goodness and opening oneself to spiritual blessings. During the seven days of Sukkot, each day is dedicated to one of the seven divine emanations (the Sefirot), starting with Chesed (kindness) and ending with Malkhut (sovereignty).

Another important ritual is the shaking of the Lulav and Etrog, which represent the unification of the different energies of the universe. By shaking them in all directions, the practitioner harmonizes the spiritual forces that sustain creation. This practice serves as a reminder that everything in the world, both on the spiritual and material planes, is interconnected.

Passover: Liberation from Inner Slavery

Passover, or Jewish Passover, marks the liberation of the Israelites from Egypt, but in Kabbalah, this liberation is also interpreted as the liberation from the inner forces that imprison the soul. Before the start of the holiday, the *Chametz* (leavened bread) must be removed from all houses, representing the purification of the ego and the spiritual impurities that grow in a disorderly manner throughout the year.

The ritual of the Passover Seder, the ceremonial meal, is full of symbolism. The Matzah, the unleavened bread, is consumed as a reminder of humility and readiness for redemption. Each of the four cups of wine drunk during the Seder represents the four expressions of liberation mentioned in the Torah, each corresponding to a divine emanation.

During the Seder, many Kabbalists meditate on the Sefirah of Tiferet, which represents beauty, harmony, and balance between spiritual forces. The goal of this meditation is to connect to the inner harmony that can emerge when the soul is freed from its spiritual chains.

Shavuot: The Reception of Divine Wisdom

Shavuot, the holiday that commemorates the giving of the Torah at Mount Sinai, is a moment of spiritual revelation. In Kabbalah, Shavuot is not just the anniversary of the Torah, but an opportunity for the practitioner to receive new levels of divine wisdom.

During the night of Shavuot, it is customary to practice *Tikkun Leil Shavuot*, a continuous study of the Torah that goes from sunset to dawn. This study is seen as a way to open the mind and heart to the light of divine wisdom. Every word studied and meditated upon during this night is like a spiritual seed that will blossom throughout the year.

The meditative practice on Shavuot is centered on the Sefirah of Binah, the emanation of understanding and deep insight. Throughout the holiday, practitioners reflect on how to integrate the learning of the Torah into their daily lives, allowing divine wisdom to shape their actions and decisions.

The Cycle of Spiritual Elevation

The Jewish holidays, as seen through Kabbalah, offer more than simple religious celebrations; they are opportunities to access divine energies that can purify, transform, and elevate the soul. By practicing the Kabbalistic rituals and meditations associated with these holidays, the practitioner can tune into the cosmic and spiritual cycles that permeate the year. Thus, each holiday is a step towards personal and collective redemption, part of a path that aims at continuous spiritual elevation.

Chapter 17
The Power of Hebrew Letters

In Kabbalah, the Hebrew alphabet plays a central role in the creation of the universe and in divine communication. Each letter is more than a linguistic symbol; it is a creative force, with specific spiritual energy and the ability to influence the physical and spiritual worlds. For Kabbalists, the Hebrew letters were not simply invented by human beings, but rather revealed as a mystical code that contains the secrets of creation and of existence itself.

The Hebrew letters are intrinsically linked to the creation of the universe, as described in the Sefer Yetzirah (Book of Creation). This sacred text teaches that God used the 22 letters of the Hebrew alphabet as building blocks to shape all realities. Each letter carries a specific energy that, when combined with other letters, produces various forms of manifestation.

In addition to being associated with creative forces, the letters are also linked to the Sephirot, the ten divine emanations that sustain the universe. This connection makes the letters powerful spiritual tools, used in meditative practices and Kabbalistic rituals.

Letters as Bridges Between the Physical and Spiritual Worlds

Each of the 22 Hebrew letters has a numerical value, a form, and a sound, all of which play specific roles in the energy they transmit. Through their numerical values, the letters connect to the practice of Gematria, the Kabbalistic system that seeks to reveal the hidden meanings behind numbers and words.

For example, the letter Aleph (א), which is the first letter of the alphabet, has the numerical value of 1. This number symbolizes the unity of God, the primordial force that precedes all creation. Aleph is seen as a silent letter, as it has no sound of its own. This represents the silence before creation, the state of absolute potential.

On the other hand, the letter Bet (ב), which comes right after Aleph and has the numerical value of 2, is associated with duality and manifestation. While Aleph represents the one, the unmanifested divine principle, Bet is the symbol of two, the beginning of creation and the separation between opposing energies—light and darkness, masculine and feminine, spiritual and material.

The form of each letter also carries a mystical meaning. In the case of Aleph, its structure combines an inclined Vav (ו) with two Yods (י), one above and one below. This reflects the balance between heaven and earth, the divine and the human. The forms of the letters can be seen as spiritual maps that represent invisible connections between the upper and lower worlds.

The sound of each letter is also fundamental to its spiritual function. Sound is considered a direct expression of divine creative energy. Reciting the letters with intention, whether in prayers or meditations, is a powerful way to connect with these energies.

The Letter Yod and the Cycle of Creation

One of the most important and revered letters in Kabbalah is Yod (י), the smallest letter of the Hebrew alphabet, but one that contains profound meanings. With the numerical value of 10, Yod symbolizes the starting point of all creation. It is said that all other letters and forms derive from this simple point, making Yod the basis of everything.

In Kabbalah, Yod is closely linked to the Sephirah of Chochmah, the emanation of divine wisdom. This association is significant, as Chochmah is the initial stage of creation, the spark of inspiration that arises before complete manifestation. Being the smallest of the letters, Yod is also seen as a symbol of humility, suggesting that true wisdom comes from the ability to be small, to nullify oneself before the divine.

The Letter Shin and Transformation

Another crucial letter in Kabbalah is Shin (ש), which is often associated with fire, transformation, and intense spiritual energy. Its numerical value is 300, a number that represents the expansive power of transformation and multiplicity.

The form of the letter Shin, with its three stems pointing to the sky, is a symbol of spiritual elevation. These three stems also represent the three columns of the Kabbalistic Tree of Life: Chesed (kindness),

Gevurah (strength), and Tiferet (harmony). Thus, Shin is a reminder of the need for balance and integration between the opposing forces of creation.

In the Tetragrammaton, the four-letter Divine Name (YHVH), the letter Shin is often seen as a symbol of the divine energy that permeates and sustains the universe. Meditating on the letter Shin can help the practitioner to transform spiritual limitations and to access higher levels of consciousness.

The Creative Power of the Word

In Kabbalah, Hebrew letters become even more powerful when combined into words. Each word, composed of a sequence of letters, is seen as a way of manifesting different aspects of creation. This means that Hebrew words—especially the Divine Names—possess an extraordinary creative force.

The word Emet (תמא), for example, which means "truth", is formed by the letters Aleph (א), Mem (מ), and Tav (ת), which are the first, middle, and last letters of the Hebrew alphabet. This symbolizes that truth encompasses the beginning, middle, and end of all creation. Truth is the divine principle that sustains and permeates all levels of existence.

Another example is the word Chai (יח), which means "life". Composed of the letters Chet (ח) and Yod (י), this word not only reflects the life force that sustains all beings, but also carries a connotation of dynamism and continuous change. In Kabbalistic practice, meditating on the word Chai can awaken energies of renewal and vitality.

Meditating on the Hebrew Letters

The practice of meditating on the Hebrew letters is one of the most powerful ways to access the spiritual energies contained in each of them. Kabbalists visualize the letters in their minds, observing their forms and reflecting on their spiritual meanings. By doing so, they come into direct contact with the creative forces that sustain the universe.

An example of this practice is meditation on the letter Hei (ה), which is linked to the Sephirah of Binah and the concept of creation from nothing. Hei is seen as the door through which souls enter the physical world. By meditating on the open form of this letter, the practitioner visualizes this passage and reflects on the interconnection between the spiritual and material worlds.

Another common practice is meditation on Aleph, which symbolizes divine unity. By visualizing Aleph and its balance between the upper and lower worlds, the practitioner seeks to align with this cosmic harmony.

The Influence of Letters in Daily Life

In addition to being used in meditations and spiritual practices, Hebrew letters also influence daily life in subtle and powerful ways. For example, choosing a Hebrew name carries great importance. A name is not just an identification, but a reflection of a person's soul and spiritual mission. Kabbalists often analyze someone's name through Gematria, revealing insights about the person's destiny and spiritual qualities.

The letters are also used in amulets and spiritual protections. Certain combinations of letters are seen as powerful spiritual shields, capable of warding off negative energies and attracting blessings. This demonstrates how letters can be used to create concrete changes in the physical world.

The Hebrew alphabet is more than a simple language; it is a mystical tool with the power to transform reality. Each letter carries with it a unique energy, linked to creation and divine manifestation. By studying and meditating on the Hebrew letters, the practitioner of Kabbalah can align with these creative forces and open doors to deeper levels of consciousness and spirituality.

In deepening the study of Hebrew letters, we will explore how to apply the knowledge of these mystical energies in a practical way, both in meditations and in personal transformations. Hebrew letters are not just symbols of an alphabet, but powerful spiritual vehicles that can be used to create, modify, and influence the practitioner's internal and external realities. Kabbalah teaches that by consciously connecting with these letters, we can unlock hidden potentials within ourselves and transform our lives.

Visualization of Hebrew Letters

One of the most effective ways to work with Hebrew letters is through visualization. Kabbalists use this practice to invoke the spiritual energy contained in each letter and apply it directly to their lives.

When visualizing a letter, the practitioner should begin by focusing on its specific form and how that form reflects its spiritual meaning. For example, meditating on the letter Aleph involves visualizing its structure—the diagonal line of Vav (ו) and the two Yods

(י) at the ends—and reflecting on the connection between the upper spiritual world and the lower material world. This process can be compared to a type of geometric meditation, where each line and curve of the letter is a symbol of a greater spiritual principle.

In addition to the form, the practitioner should pay attention to the sound of the letter, if it has a sound, or to its absence, as in the case of Aleph. The sound of the letters, as mentioned earlier, represents a creative manifestation of the divine, and reciting the letters aloud or internally can help bring the letter's energy into the present moment. The repetition of the sound, in a slow and rhythmic manner, is often used to anchor consciousness in a heightened state of connection with spiritual forces.

Meditation on the Tetragrammaton: YHVH

One of the most profound examples of how letters can be used in meditation is the Kabbalistic practice of visualizing the Tetragrammaton, the Divine Name formed by the letters Yod (י), Hei (ה), Vav (ו), and Hei (ה). This name, which is considered the most sacred of all, represents the divine essence and the creative force that permeates all existence.

Meditation on the Tetragrammaton involves several stages of visualization and reflection:

Yod (י): Represents the starting point of creation, the spark of divine consciousness. By visualizing Yod, the practitioner connects with the divine aspect that is beyond any physical form, the pure energy of creative potential.

Hei (ה): The first Hei represents the stage of expansion and manifestation from this initial point. It is the "breath" of creation, the formation of an idea or concept. Visualizing Hei is to connect with the process of giving form to what was previously unmanifested.

Vav (ו): This letter symbolizes the channel through which spiritual energy flows from the divine world to the material world. When meditating on the letter Vav, the practitioner imagines this energy flowing into physical reality, establishing a bridge between the spiritual and the material.

Hei (ה): The second Hei completes the cycle of creation, bringing spiritual energy fully into the physical world. Visualizing this final letter is to visualize the complete manifestation of creation in its most tangible and concrete form.

The practice of these visualizations is not merely theoretical; it aims to align the practitioner with the divine principles that govern creation. By working consistently with the Tetragrammaton, it is possible to tune into the cycles of creation and manifestation that occur both in the universe and within each individual.

The Use of Hebrew Letters for Personal Transformation

The application of Hebrew letters goes beyond static meditation. They can be used to promote profound personal transformations. Each letter represents a spiritual quality that can be cultivated or awakened in the practitioner, depending on their needs and challenges.

For example, a person who is facing challenges related to self-expression can focus on the letter Peh (פ), which is associated with the mouth and the ability to communicate. Meditation and recitation of Peh can help release blockages related to speech, allowing the person to express themselves with greater clarity and sincerity.

Similarly, someone who is seeking more willpower or resilience can meditate on the letter Tav (ת), which is the last letter of the alphabet and symbolizes completion and determination. Tav also represents the end of a cycle, which can be useful for those who are seeking to complete a project or overcome a difficult phase in their lives.

The Composition of Names: Personal and Divine Energy

Another important practice that involves Hebrew letters is the study and meditation on names—both Divine Names and personal names. In the Kabbalistic tradition, names are not mere labels, but expressions of an individual's essence and spiritual mission. Each letter of a name contributes a specific energy that shapes the person's character and destiny.

The practice of meditating on one's own name or on sacred names is a way to activate these energies and integrate their potentials into daily life. For example, the Hebrew name Moses (Moshe, משה) is composed of the letters Mem (מ), Shin (ש), and Hei (ה). Each of these letters carries a profound meaning: Mem is associated with water and fluid wisdom, Shin with fire and transformation, and Hei with the process of revelation.

Meditating on this name can help awaken these qualities and understand them more deeply.

In addition, Kabbalists also believe that meditating on the Divine Names can bring protection and guidance. The combination of letters in the name Elohim (מיהלא), for example, contains powerful meanings associated with strength, justice, and judgment. By connecting with these letters through meditation, the practitioner can access these divine qualities in times of need.

Practices of Chanting and Recitation

Another powerful method of working with Hebrew letters is the chanting or recitation of the letters. This method, known as Hitbodedut or Hitbonenut, involves the repetition of specific sounds and words to induce a heightened state of spiritual consciousness.

By reciting the letters in sequence or repeating a single letter as a mantra, the practitioner activates the vibrational power of the letter, allowing its energy to permeate the mind, body, and spirit. This practice can be performed silently or aloud, depending on the intention. When chanted aloud, the vibration of the letters can have a tangible physical impact, harmonizing internal and external energies.

The letter Shin, for example, which has already been mentioned as associated with fire, can be recited repeatedly to activate a sense of vitality and transformation. Similarly, the repetition of the letter Yod can help access a state of inner wisdom and mental clarity.

Exercises for Working with the Letters

To integrate this knowledge into a daily practice, here are some practical exercises you can do to work with the Hebrew letters and access their transformative energies:

Daily Visualization of a Letter: Choose one letter per day to meditate on. Visualize its form, its color (according to your intuition), and repeat the sound of the letter slowly. Reflect on how the energy of this letter can be applied in your current life.

Meditation on Your Own Name: Write your name in Hebrew and visualize each letter separately. Reflect on how each letter influences your character and mission. What can each one reveal about your gifts and challenges?

Chanting of Letter Mantras: Choose a letter that you feel you need to work on, such as Shin for transformation or Peh for communication. Recite this letter repeatedly in a monotone, focusing on the sound and vibration it creates in your body.

Analysis of Names: Apply the principles of Gematria to analyze the names of people or words important in your life. What do the numerical values reveal about their spiritual and energetic connections?

Hebrew letters are much more than simple characters; they are powerful spiritual tools that can bring transformation on profound levels. Working with these letters, whether through meditation, recitation, or visualization, allows the practitioner to access a vast source of creative and spiritual energy, aligning with the forces that shape the universe. With consistent practice, these letters can open doors to new levels of understanding, healing, and spiritual development.

Chapter 18
Kabbalah and Dreams

Dreams play a significant role in Kabbalah, being considered direct messages from the unconscious and the spiritual world. Since ancient times, Kabbalists believed that dreams were more than just mental activities during sleep; they are communication channels between the soul and the higher dimensions. Through dreams, the spiritual world can reveal secrets, give guidance, and even allow the soul to access higher levels of consciousness. Kabbalah teaches that, during sleep, the human soul goes on a journey. Part of the soul, mainly the Nefesh (the most basic level of the soul), remains in the body, while the Ruach and Neshamah (the emotional and spiritual levels of the soul) can ascend to the spiritual worlds. In doing so, the soul comes into contact with divine forces, angels, and other spiritual entities that reside in different planes of creation. It is during these moments that the soul can receive revelations and insights that, upon returning to the body, manifest in the form of dreams.

Types of Dreams in Kabbalah

Kabbalah classifies dreams into different categories, according to their spiritual origins and their contents. These classifications help to discern the nature and relevance of each dream, as not all dreams are the same. Some may be divine messages, while others may simply reflect the anxieties and concerns of everyday life.

Prophetic Dreams: These are dreams that come directly from the divine or spiritual worlds. They bring clear and symbolic messages, often involving sacred figures or spiritual archetypes. Kabbalists believe that great prophets, like Joseph in Egypt, received important messages through this type of dream. These dreams are rare and may contain guidance for important decisions, revelations about destiny, or even about future events.

Psychological Dreams: Unlike prophetic dreams, psychological dreams are an expression of the dreamer's unconscious emotions, thoughts, and desires. They can be reflections of tensions, fears, or anxieties that the individual is facing in their waking life. In Kabbalah, these dreams are considered less spiritual, but they can still be valuable, as they reveal internal states that need to be addressed or balanced.

Mystical or Spiritual Dreams: These dreams are between the prophetic and the psychological. They are not direct messages from the divine, but they are spiritual journeys that the soul takes while the body rests. During these dreams, the soul may encounter spiritual beings, travel through different levels of reality, or receive insights into personal and spiritual matters. These dreams are often rich in symbolism and can be difficult to interpret without a deep understanding of Kabbalistic principles.

Symbolism in Dreams

Symbolism plays a crucial role in the interpretation of Kabbalistic dreams. Each element of the dream, whether it is an object, a color, a person, or an event, has a specific meaning that can be deciphered to reveal the hidden spiritual content. The symbols in dreams are ways through which spiritual messages, often complex and subtle, are transmitted to the dreamer.

In Kabbalah, some of the most common symbols include:

Water: Symbolizes wisdom and spiritual knowledge. A dream involving water may indicate that the dreamer is seeking more wisdom or is in a process of spiritual purification. The form that water takes in the dream is also important: clean water can represent spiritual clarity, while dirty water can indicate confusion or negative emotions.

Trees: Trees generally symbolize the Tree of Life, and dreams involving trees may be related to spiritual growth, connection with the Sephirot, or even the physical and emotional health of the dreamer. Dreaming of healthy and flowering trees can be a sign of prosperity and spiritual well-being.

Light: Light is often associated with divine presence and spiritual revelation. A dream where light plays an important role may indicate that the dreamer is receiving guidance or is approaching a new level of spiritual understanding.

Fire: Fire is a symbol of purification and transformation, and in dreams, it can represent a need for change or to eliminate something negative from the dreamer's life. However, it can also be a symbol of destruction, depending on the context of the dream.

Animals: Different animals can have different meanings, and their interpretation depends on both the animal itself and its behavior in the dream. For example, a snake can be a symbol of healing and transformation, while a lion can represent power and protection.

The Technique of Dream Interpretation

Kabbalists developed detailed methods for interpreting dreams. One of the best-known techniques is Hitbonenut, which involves meditation and deep reflection on the symbols present in the dream. Through this practice, the dreamer can unfold the hidden meanings behind the elements of the dream.

First, the dreamer should record the dream immediately after waking up, as the details tend to fade quickly. Writing down the symbols and emotions experienced in the dream is crucial for interpretation. The next step is to meditate on these symbols, connecting them with the Kabbalistic teachings that relate to them. For example, when dreaming of water, the dreamer can meditate on the Sephirah of Chochmah, which represents wisdom, and consider how the dream aligns with their state of seeking wisdom in waking life.

In addition, some Kabbalists recommend consulting with a spiritual master or someone experienced in interpreting dreams. This is because, often, the correct interpretation of a dream may require a deeper and more trained eye, capable of deciphering nuances that the dreamer alone may not perceive.

Dreams and the Tree of Life

One of the most fascinating aspects of the Kabbalistic view of dreams is the relationship between dreams and the Tree of Life. During sleep, the dreamer's soul can ascend through the different Sephirot of the Tree of Life, receiving insights and experiences according to the spiritual level it reaches.

Assiyah (Action): If the dream occurs at the level of Assiyah, it may be related to practical and material issues of waking life. These dreams are often more connected to everyday reality and less spiritual.

Yetzirah (Formation): At the level of Yetzirah, dreams may focus on emotional issues and relationships. The symbols may reveal repressed feelings or unresolved traumas.

Beriah (Creation): Dreams that occur at the level of Beriah tend to be more spiritual and philosophical, bringing messages about the purpose of life or deeper questions of existence.

Atzilut (Emanation): This is the highest level and rarely reached in dreams. When a dream occurs in Atzilut, it can be an experience of union with the divine, where the dreamer connects directly with the source of creation.

The Meaning of Nightmares

Nightmares are also addressed in Kabbalah as phenomena that can have important spiritual meanings. They are often seen as reflections of tensions or internal conflicts that need to be resolved. However, they can also be manifestations of external energies or negative forces that surround the dreamer.

Kabbalists believe that, when experiencing a nightmare, the dreamer should carefully analyze their emotions and spiritual state. Recurring nightmares can be a sign that something in their life needs attention or healing. The practice of Tikun—spiritual correction—can be used to address the emotional or spiritual aspects that nightmares reveal.

Practical Exercises for Dream Recall

For those who wish to start working more deeply with dreams, Kabbalah suggests some simple but powerful practices to help recall and interpret dreams.

Intention before sleep: Before falling asleep, it is helpful to set a clear intention, such as a request to receive spiritual guidance or clarity on a specific issue. This practice can increase the likelihood of having a meaningful dream.

Dream Journal: Keep a journal by the bedside to record dreams immediately upon waking. Write down as many details as possible, including symbols, colors, and emotions felt during the dream.

Prayer for Dream Recall: Some Kabbalists recommend a short prayer before sleeping, asking to remember dreams and receive spiritual insights through them.

Dreams, in Kabbalah, are portals to spiritual dimensions and inner revelations. By understanding the structure of dreams and the symbols they contain, we can begin to consciously work with these altered states of consciousness and use the messages of dreams for our spiritual growth. After understanding the importance of dreams in Kabbalah and the role they play as spiritual portals, the next step is to learn how to increase the clarity of these dreams and master the techniques of interpretation. Kabbalistic practice involves more than just the recognition of dream symbols; it offers a set of tools to explore dreams consciously and extract meaningful spiritual information.

Techniques to Increase Dream Clarity

One of the main challenges that many people face when working with their dreams is the lack of clarity. Often, dreams can seem confusing, fragmented, or difficult to remember. However, Kabbalah teaches that there are ways to train the mind and spirit to remember and interpret dreams more effectively.

1. Mental and Spiritual Preparation Before Sleep

Dream clarity can be influenced by spiritual and mental preparation before sleep. In Kabbalah, the idea of Hitbonenut (meditation) is central to calming the mind and opening the soul to spiritual messages during sleep. Taking time to meditate before bed, focusing on calming thoughts, can create a more receptive environment for dreams.

Another recommended practice is to recite Psalms or other sacred prayers before sleep. These texts are considered protective and purifying, helping to ward off negative energies and creating an opening for dreams to be clearer and spiritually guided. A simple prayer can be made with the intention of receiving spiritual guidance during sleep, such as:

"O Source of Wisdom and Light, I ask for Your guidance and protection during my sleep. May my soul receive Your messages and may I have clarity to understand the symbols and teachings that will be revealed to me. Amen."

2. Purification of the Sleep Environment

The physical environment where we sleep also has a significant impact on dream clarity. According to Kabbalistic teachings, spiritual energies flow through physical spaces, and therefore, it is important to keep the place where one sleeps free of negative energies. The practice of purifying the space can be done in various ways, such as:

Physical and spiritual cleaning of the room: Keeping the space clean, organized, and quiet helps promote a healthy sleep environment. In addition, the use of spiritual elements, such as burning incense, can be a way to purify the environment. Myrrh or frankincense is often used by Kabbalists to elevate the spiritual energy of the space.

Placement of sacred symbols: Some Kabbalists recommend keeping a symbol of the Tree of Life or a scroll containing verses from the Torah near the bed. This creates a direct connection with divine energy during sleep.

3. Setting a Clear Intention

In Kabbalah, intention, or kavanah, is crucial in any spiritual practice, and this applies to dreams. Setting a clear intention before sleep directs the spiritual energy and attention of the soul to a specific area. This can be done through a short meditation or a simple affirmation, asking for guidance or clarity on a specific issue.

For example, if someone is seeking an answer or guidance on a dilemma, they can focus on this thought before falling asleep, repeating an affirmation such as: "I ask for clarity and understanding about [specific issue]." This act of directing intention helps to open the channel of communication between the dreamer and the spiritual realms.

4. Exercises to Improve Dream Recall

The ability to remember dreams is an essential step to interpreting and working with them. Some Kabbalists practice the use of a dream journal, writing down what they remember as soon as they wake up. This strengthens the ability to recall dreams and increases awareness of the symbols and themes that arise.

Another practical exercise is to focus on the sensory details of dreams—the colors, sounds, textures, and even the emotions experienced during the dream. The more details are recorded, the easier the subsequent interpretation will be. For those who have difficulty remembering dreams, a simple technique is to say to oneself, before sleeping: "I will remember my dreams when I wake up." This internal repetition programs the mind to pay more attention to dreams.

5. Morning Meditation

The practice of a short meditation soon after waking up can help to further clarify the symbols and messages of dreams. In the moment between sleep and complete awakening, the mind is still connected to the spiritual world. Sitting in silence and reflecting on what was dreamed can bring to light new information or aspects of the dream that were not initially perceived.

A powerful technique is to focus attention on the most striking symbol or event of the dream and meditate on it, asking for spiritual guidance to understand its meaning. For example, if the dreamer dreamed of a bright light, they can meditate on the energy of light, asking: "What is this light trying to reveal to me?"

Kabbalistic Methods of Dream Interpretation

Dream interpretation in Kabbalah is a complex process that involves both the study of symbols and spiritual intuition. Here are some of the most commonly used Kabbalistic methods for interpreting dreams:

1. Symbolism of the Tree of Life

Kabbalists often use the Tree of Life as a map to interpret dreams. Each Sephirah represents a specific quality or aspect of the spiritual world, and the symbols in dreams may be related to these Sephirot.

For example, if someone dreams of a ladder, this symbol can be interpreted as a representation of the soul's ascent through the Sephirot, towards a greater understanding of the divine. If the ladder is clear and easily climbable, it may indicate spiritual progress; if it is difficult or broken, it may represent blockages or challenges that need to be overcome.

2. Interpretation of Numbers and Names

Gematria, the Kabbalistic system of numerology, is also used to interpret the numbers that appear in dreams. Each number has a spiritual value, and its meaning can be revealed by deciphering it in the light of Gematria. For example, the number 10 is associated with totality and completeness, as it is the number of the

Sephirot. Dreaming of this number may indicate that the dreamer is close to achieving an important spiritual goal.

Similarly, the names that appear in dreams can have hidden meanings when viewed through the lens of Gematria. The name of a person or place in the dream can reveal more about their purpose or spiritual function.

3. Meaning of Colors

Colors also play an important role in the interpretation of Kabbalistic dreams. Each color has a correspondence with the Sephirot and with specific spiritual energies. Here are some common examples:

White: Purity, clarity, the presence of God (related to the Sephirah of Keter).

Red: Passion, judgment, strength (related to the Sephirah of Gevurah).

Green: Growth, balance, harmony (related to the Sephirah of Tiferet).

Blue: Wisdom, elevated spirituality (related to the Sephirah of Chochmah).

The predominant color in a dream can give clues about the nature of the spiritual message. A dream shrouded in white may suggest that the dreamer is in a state of purity or is receiving a direct message from the divine.

Practice of Lucid Dreams

Kabbalah also recognizes the importance of lucid dreams—the ability to be aware that one is dreaming and, in some cases, control the dream. In lucid dreams, the dreamer can consciously explore the spiritual world, ask questions, and even seek guidance directly from spiritual beings.

To cultivate the ability to dream lucidly, Kabbalists recommend maintaining a regular practice of meditation, cultivating self-awareness during the day. This helps to increase lucidity during the dream state. In addition, repeating a mantra or intention before sleep, such as "I will recognize that I am dreaming," can help induce lucid dreams.

When in a lucid dream, the dreamer can take the opportunity to directly ask the symbols of the dream for their meaning. For example, if a mysterious figure appears, the dreamer can ask: "Who are you and what do you represent?" This conscious interaction with the content of the dream can reveal deeper and more immediate answers.

Dreams and Spiritual Healing

Another powerful aspect of dreams, according to Kabbalah, is their ability to offer spiritual healing. Through dreams, the soul can work to process and heal traumas, repressed emotions, or spiritual blockages. Kabbalists believe that many of our emotional and spiritual problems can be resolved during the dream state, when we are more open to healing energies.

To promote this healing, it is helpful to maintain an attitude of acceptance and receptivity to dreams, trusting that they have the potential to reveal what needs to be transformed.

Chapter 19
The Path of Repentance
Teshuvah in Kabbalah

In Kabbalah, the concept of Teshuvah, or repentance, goes beyond mere confession of errors and requests for forgiveness. It is a profound process of spiritual return to the state of unity with the Divinity, repairing spiritual flaws and realigning with the soul's higher purpose. The word Teshuvah comes from the Hebrew root "shuv," which means "to return." Thus, Teshuvah is the process of "returning" to our true spiritual essence and correcting the deviations that have distanced us from our connection with the divine. Kabbalah teaches that repentance is a necessary path for every human being, as imperfections and flaws are part of the spiritual journey. There is no evolution without mistakes and without the conscious effort to correct them. In the Kabbalistic view, Teshuvah is not only a response to sins but an opportunity for spiritual growth and refinement, allowing the soul to reach a higher level of connection with the Creator.

Repentance in the Creation of the World

To understand the fundamental role of Teshuvah, it is important to look at its position in the process of creation. Kabbalah teaches that the concept of repentance was created even before the creation of the world. This means that, in the divine plan itself, there was the foresight that human beings would make mistakes and would need a way to redeem themselves and reconnect with the divine. The world was created intentionally imperfect, with room for human flaws, so that, through Teshuvah, these flaws could be corrected and the world could be constantly elevated. Every time an individual does Teshuvah, they not only correct their own soul but also contribute to the rectification and elevation of the entire world, collaborating in the process of Tikun Olam, or correction of the universe.

The Four Stages of Teshuvah

In the Kabbalistic tradition, the process of Teshuvah is described as having four main stages. Each of these stages reflects an aspect of the inner journey of repentance and transformation, providing a clear guide for those who wish to walk this path.

1. Recognition of the Error

The first step of Teshuvah is to recognize the mistake made. This recognition must come from a sincere and honest awareness of the actions, thoughts, or words that have diverted the person from the spiritual path. However, it is not enough to just admit the mistake superficially. It is necessary to meditate deeply on how this flaw affected the spiritual balance, both on a personal and cosmic level. In Kabbalah, this recognition is also seen as a way to illuminate the darkness. When a mistake is recognized, it is brought to the light of consciousness, where it can be analyzed and understood.

This prevents the error from remaining hidden and continuing to exert a negative influence on the soul.

2. Sincere Remorse

After recognizing the error, the next step is to feel deep and sincere remorse for having committed it. This repentance should not be confused with guilt or shame, feelings that can often paralyze spiritual progress. Remorse in Kabbalah is a positive emotion, as it is the awakening of the soul to its true nature and the desire to return to the state of purity. Sincere remorse is not about emotional punishment, but rather a transformative force that awakens the will to change. It must be accompanied by a deep understanding that, despite the mistake made, there is always the possibility of correcting the path and rising spiritually.

3. Decision-Making Not to Repeat the Error

The third stage of the Teshuvah process is the firm decision not to repeat the error. This requires serious reflection on the behavior patterns that led to the deviation and the establishment of new intentions to avoid falling into the same trap. This decision must be made with complete conviction, ensuring that the person is committed to change. In Kabbalah, this stage is crucial, as it is the moment when the individual begins to rewrite their spiritual destiny. By making the conscious decision not to repeat the error, the person is, in a way, "creating" a new path for themselves. This demonstrates to the universe that there is a genuine desire for rectification, and, in response, the universe begins to reorganize circumstances to support this new purpose.

4. Act of Correction

The final stage of Teshuvah involves the concrete action of correction. This step goes beyond internal repentance; it requires the individual to do something in the external world to rectify the error. This can take many forms, depending on the nature of the error. It may involve apologizing to those who were harmed, performing good deeds to balance the negative impact, or, in deeper cases, dedicating oneself to study and spiritual practice to cleanse the spiritual energies involved.

In the Kabbalistic context, the act of correction is closely linked to the concept of Tikun Olam, because, by correcting a mistake, the person is helping to restore harmony in the universe. Each act of rectification not only heals the individual but also contributes to the healing of the world.

Teshuvah and the Four Worlds of Kabbalah

The journey of repentance can be seen through the prism of the Four Worlds of Kabbalah: Assiyah (Action), Yetzirah (Formation), Beriá (Creation), and Atzilut (Emanation). Each of these worlds represents a level of existence and spiritual consciousness, and Teshuvah can be experienced in each of them.

In the world of Assiyah, repentance manifests through physical actions. This is where practical correction happens, where the person performs acts of reparation and rectification. In the world of Yetzirah, repentance takes the form of emotions and feelings. Sincere remorse is felt at this level, awakening the desire for change and internal purification. In the world of Beriá, repentance is related to thought and intention. Here, the individual meditates on the root causes of their flaws and establishes new spiritual intentions. In the world of Atzilut, Teshuvah is experienced as a complete union with the divine. This is the highest level of repentance, where the soul returns to its pure and original state, merging with the divine light. Each level of Teshuvah corresponds to a deeper purification, allowing the soul to rise from one level to another until it reaches complete reconciliation with the Creator.

The Transformative Power of Teshuvah

In Kabbalah, Teshuvah is seen as one of the most powerful forces in the universe. There is a Kabbalistic teaching that states that "there is nothing that stands above Teshuvah." This means that, regardless of the gravity of the mistakes made, Teshuvah has the power to rectify everything and to transform even the most negative actions into opportunities for spiritual growth. One of the profound mysteries of Teshuvah is that, by doing this process of return, the individual not only redeems themselves but can transform their flaws into merits. As the Talmud teaches, "where penitents stand, even the righteous cannot stand." This means that those who have gone through the process of Teshuvah reach a higher spiritual level than those who have never erred, because they have experienced the internal transformation of their flaws. Teshuvah is also a demonstration of the unconditional love of the Creator. Kabbalah teaches that God is always waiting for the return of the soul, and that there is no limit to divine mercy. The process of repentance is, in fact, a path back to this divine love, and each step taken in this direction is received with great welcome by the higher worlds.

Daily Teshuvah

Although Teshuvah is often associated with major transgressions, Kabbalists recommend that it be practiced daily, as a way to maintain the purity of the soul and spiritual alignment. At the end of each day, the individual can reflect on their actions, thoughts, and emotions, seeking to correct any imbalance or flaw before sleeping. This practice of daily repentance helps to keep the soul in a constant state of purification, preventing flaws from accumulating and creating spiritual obstacles. The daily practice of Teshuvah not only strengthens the connection with the divine but also prepares the soul for a life of continuous spiritual growth. It allows each day to be an opportunity for renewal, where the soul can correct its deviations and walk again towards the light. With this, repentance becomes a practice not only occasional but an integral part of spiritual life, bringing constant evolution, growth, and return to the divine essence.

The process of Teshuvah is much more than a simple practice of remorse. In Kabbalah, it unfolds into deep spiritual techniques and practices, which aim not only to repair flaws but also to transform one's own life into a constant journey of return and reconnection with the Creator.

Kabbalistic Meditations for Teshuvah

Meditation is a central tool in Kabbalistic practice and plays a crucial role in the process of Teshuvah. One of the most powerful meditations for repentance is associated with the Tetragrammaton, the sacred name of God, YHVH (הוהי). By meditating on the letters of the Tetragrammaton, the Kabbalist can reconnect with the different dimensions of divinity, purifying their soul and realigning with the divine purpose.

Each letter of the Tetragrammaton represents a different aspect of existence:

Yud (י): Represents wisdom and the starting point of creation. In meditation, the practitioner reflects on the origin of their actions, seeking to understand the root of their flaws and the divine potential behind them. Hei (ה): Symbolizes the expansion of wisdom into understanding. Here, the practitioner meditates on the consequences of their actions and how these reverberate in the world around them. Vav (ו): Represents the connection between the high and the low, between the spiritual and the material. In this phase of meditation, the Kabbalist seeks to integrate spiritual learning into their practical life, committing to not repeating their mistakes. Hei (ה): The second Hei letter indicates the materialization of the divine purpose. At the end of the meditation, the practitioner visualizes their flaws being transformed into rectified actions, bringing light to the physical world.

This meditation is accompanied by specific visualizations, such as the white light that purifies and restores the soul, or the progressive ascent through the Four Worlds of Kabbalah, starting in Assiyah and ascending to Atzilut, as described previously. As the practitioner ascends through the worlds, they approach the divine essence and gradually correct the spiritual flaws that have distanced them from their path.

Prayers of Repentance and Reconciliation

Prayer is another powerful tool in the process of Teshuvah. The Kabbalistic tradition offers various prayers to help the practitioner reconnect with God and seek reparation for the flaws committed. One of the most profound prayers is the Vidui, a confession recited in moments of sincere repentance. In the Vidui, the individual openly acknowledges their flaws before God, asking for forgiveness with a contrite heart.

The Vidui is not just a list of transgressions; it is an opportunity for self-assessment and purification. By verbally confessing their mistakes, the practitioner causes their flaws to cease being unconscious or hidden, bringing them to the surface where they can be addressed. According to Kabbalah, the power of the spoken word is immense, as words shape reality. By confessing flaws, the individual begins to undo the damage caused by their actions, allowing sincere repentance to bring healing to the soul.

In addition to the Vidui, the prayers of the Psalms are frequently used in the process of Teshuvah. Specifically, Psalm 51 is a prayer of repentance that has been traditionally associated with the search for purification and forgiveness. The words "Create in me a clean heart, O God, and renew a steadfast spirit within me" are recited as a request for the Creator to help transform and renew the interior of the one who repents.

Acts of Kindness and Charity

Kabbalah teaches that Teshuvah is not complete without concrete action. This means that in addition to the recognition and confession of errors, it is necessary to act in the physical world to repair the damage caused. One of the most effective means for this rectification is the practice of acts of kindness, known as Chessed, and charity, Tzedakah.

Tzedakah is a fundamental principle in Jewish mysticism, not only as a form of material aid but as a way to rectify the spiritual imbalance caused by human flaws. When the individual practices charity, they are reversing the flow of selfishness that led to the transgression and transforming it into generosity. According to Kabbalah, the act of giving opens the channels of blessings, allowing the divine light to flow again into their life and into the world.

Chessed, in turn, involves acts of kindness that go beyond financial aid. They are actions that promote harmony, love, and support among people, being an essential part of the process of Teshuvah. When someone commits a mistake that harmed other people, it is through kindness and reconciliation that this mistake can be truly corrected. Kabbalah emphasizes that true Teshuvah can only occur when balance is restored both on the spiritual and relational levels.

Fasting and Reflection

In certain cases, fasting is recommended as a practice of self-assessment and purification during the process of Teshuvah. In the Kabbalistic tradition, fasting is not seen as a bodily punishment but as a way to elevate the soul by restricting the desires of the body.

The goal of fasting is to focus the mind and heart on spiritual realities, creating space for introspection and reconnection with God.

During the fast, the practitioner can dedicate themselves to prayer, study, and meditation, seeking a higher state of spiritual consciousness. Fasting is also an opportunity for the Kabbalist to reflect deeply on their actions and motivations, immersing themselves in the process of Teshuvah with greater intensity and clarity. Traditionally, fasting is combined with the recitation of the Psalms and other prayers that help to elevate the spirit and purify the body.

Teshuvah and the Balance of the Sefirot

The practice of Teshuvah is often associated with rebalancing the Sefirot within the soul. Each Sefirah corresponds to a specific spiritual quality, and often, human deviations and transgressions are related to an imbalance in these qualities. For example, if someone commits a mistake because of anger, this may indicate an imbalance in the Sefirah of Gevurah, which is associated with rigor and justice. Similarly, mistakes committed through excessive indulgence may reflect an imbalance in Chessed, the Sefirah of love and kindness.

The process of Teshuvah involves identifying where the imbalance in the Sefirot occurred and then working to restore harmony. This can be done through specific meditations, such as the aforementioned meditation on the Tetragrammaton, or through practices that strengthen the quality that is lacking. If the error was related to a lack of self-control, for example, one can meditate on the energy of Gevurah to restore balance. If the problem was coldness or emotional detachment, meditation on the energy of Chessed can be useful to open the heart and re-establish the flow of kindness.

Teshuvah as Spiritual Rebirth

Kabbalah teaches that Teshuvah has the power to bring a spiritual rebirth to the soul. After completing the process of repentance, the soul is considered renewed, as if it had returned to its original state of purity. This reflects the idea that repentance not only "erases" transgressions but profoundly transforms the essence of the person.

This transformation is described as a true rebirth. The soul, which was previously obscured by errors, now shines with more intensity, as it has passed through the furnace of spiritual purification. Thus, the practitioner who completes Teshuvah becomes a more elevated human being, with greater spiritual clarity, moral strength, and proximity to the Creator.

Continuity and Constancy in the Path of Teshuvah

One of the most important aspects of Teshuvah is its continuity. Kabbalah does not see repentance as a one-time event but as a constant process, which should accompany the individual throughout their entire spiritual journey. Daily, the practitioner is encouraged to reflect on their actions, words, and thoughts, seeking to correct small deviations before they become large obstacles.

The constant practice of Teshuvah helps the soul to remain in harmony with the divine purpose. It prevents errors from accumulating and turning into spiritual burdens, allowing the individual to continue growing and rising spiritually. Constancy in repentance is one of the secrets of spiritual evolution in Kabbalah, as it keeps the soul always open to the divine light.

Teshuvah is, undoubtedly, one of the most profound and transformative processes of Kabbalah. It teaches that no matter how far we may feel from the divine light, there is always a way back, and this path is illuminated by sincere repentance, the correction of errors, and the renewal of the soul. By practicing Teshuvah consciously and constantly, the individual aligns with the cosmic forces of correction and redemption, bringing harmony to their own life and to the world around them.

Chapter 20
Kabbalah and the Role of Women

In Kabbalah, the role of women is seen in a profound and central way, with a particular emphasis on the connection with divine feminine energies. Unlike traditional approaches that often relegate the feminine to a secondary role, Kabbalistic mysticism recognizes and reveres the creative and spiritual force inherent in women, considering them as bearers of a special connection with the Divinity.

The Shechinah: The Divine Feminine Presence

At the heart of Kabbalah, the Shechinah is the manifestation of the divine presence that dwells in the world. She is often described as the feminine aspect of God, the part of the divinity that is closest to human beings, guiding and protecting them. The Shechinah is seen as the presence of God in the physical universe and in mundane affairs, connecting heaven and earth.

The Shechinah is not just an abstract concept, but a dynamic and interactive aspect of divinity. She is associated with compassion, protection, and nurturing, acting as the "cosmic mother" who sustains the world and its creatures. At the same time, the Shechinah also suffers when humanity turns away from the divinity, as in cases of injustice and spiritual impurity. When people commit acts of disharmony, they "exile" the Shechinah, distancing her from the world and causing a separation between the divine and the human.

Within this context, women, according to Kabbalah, have a special affinity with the Shechinah. Kabbalists teach that women, in their very essence, are a microcosmic manifestation of this divine feminine presence. This means that women, in their natural role, possess a unique spiritual sensitivity and an innate power to bring light and harmony to the world, reconnecting the Shechinah with material reality.

The Divine Feminine and Creation

In Kabbalistic mysticism, the process of creation is often described in terms of masculine and feminine energies working together. The Sefirot, which represent the divine emanations, contain both masculine and feminine elements. The interaction between these energies is essential for the balanced functioning of the universe.

The Sefirah of Binah, for example, is traditionally associated with the feminine. It represents understanding, the ability to nurture and give form to what was conceived by the Sefirah of Chochmah, which represents wisdom. While Chochmah plants the "seed" of the idea, Binah develops it, transforming it into a concrete reality. This process is seen as analogous to gestation and birth in the physical world, where women play the central role of nurturing and giving life.

Furthermore, Binah is deeply connected to intuition, another quality associated with the feminine in Kabbalah. Intuition is seen as a form of knowledge that transcends logical and linear reasoning, allowing the soul to access deeper and subtler spiritual truths. This intuitive ability, valued in the Kabbalistic tradition, is considered one of the most powerful contributions of women to the spiritual balance of the universe.

Women as Guardians of the Home and the Sacred

In the physical world, women have traditionally been associated with the home and family, but Kabbalah sees this role as much more than merely domestic. In the Kabbalistic view, the home is a sacred space, where the divine presence can be attracted and manifested, and women are considered primarily responsible for creating and maintaining this sanctity in the physical space.

Tradition teaches that women's daily spiritual practices—from lighting the Shabbat candles to keeping Kosher (dietary laws)—are ways of attracting the Shechinah to the home. The lighting of the Shabbat candles, in particular, is seen as a moment when women illuminate the spiritual and physical world, bringing peace and the divine presence to their home. In fact, Shabbat itself is personified in Kabbalah as a bride or queen, a feminine figure who symbolizes the union between the divine and the world.

Moreover, Kabbalah teaches that women have a special power in their words and actions to influence the spiritual environment around them. Their role as mother, wife, and caregiver is not just a social responsibility, but an elevated spiritual function that directly impacts the cosmic balance. By sustaining harmony and purity in their home, women are, in fact, helping to bring balance to the spiritual forces of the universe.

The Secret Wisdom of Women

The Kabbalistic tradition recognizes that women possess a unique spiritual wisdom, often called *Binat Halev*, "the understanding of the heart." This wisdom is a form of spiritual intuition that allows women to perceive hidden truths and access levels of understanding that may not be immediately apparent to others. This "wisdom of the heart" is seen as a divine gift that allows women to exercise a role of spiritual leadership, especially within their family and community.

In Kabbalah, women are often seen as holders of a silent but powerful spiritual force. It is not uncommon for the stories of great Kabbalists to be accompanied by accounts of the women in their lives—wives, mothers, daughters—who played fundamental roles in their spiritual development. These women often served as counselors and spiritual guides, helping their husbands or sons reach higher levels of understanding.

The Balance of Masculine and Feminine Energies

Kabbalah emphasizes the importance of balance between masculine and feminine energies, both in the external world and within each individual. Although each human being has their own proportion of masculine and feminine energies, women are seen as naturally more attuned to the feminine energies of creation. However, this balance does not mean that one energy should suppress the other; on the contrary, true harmony is achieved when both energies work together.

Kabbalistic spiritual practices often involve meditation on these energies and their integration into daily life. For example, in morning prayers or meditations on the Tree of Life, the practitioner seeks to harmonize within themselves the qualities of Chesed (kindness, generally associated with the feminine) and Gevurah (strength, generally associated with the masculine). Women, in particular, are seen as experts in manifesting Chesed, bringing the energy of compassion and nurturing to the world.

Women and Spiritual Transmission

Another essential aspect of the role of women in Kabbalah is their function as transmitters of spirituality to future generations. This is not limited to the role of biological mother, but includes any form of teaching, guidance, and spiritual leadership that women exercise in their community. Kabbalah deeply values the role of women in the spiritual education of their children and in creating an environment that fosters spiritual growth.

By transmitting spiritual values, women become a bridge between the physical and spiritual worlds, ensuring that the light of Kabbalah and mysticism continues to shine from generation to generation. This function of transmitting divine wisdom is more than a simple act of teaching; it is an act of creating and perpetuating the divine presence in the world.

The role of women in Kabbalah goes far beyond the superficial conventions that are often attributed to the feminine. She is seen as a figure of spiritual strength, endowed with a special connection to the divine energies and the Shechinah. Her power lies in her ability to nurture, protect, and illuminate both on the spiritual and physical levels, becoming a guardian of sacred traditions and a conductor of divine light in the world.

By recognizing and honoring her role, Kabbalah offers women a position of profound reverence and importance within the cosmic scheme, highlighting the interdependence between masculine and feminine energies and the importance of both for the realization of the divine purpose.

Understanding the central role of women in Kabbalah, it is important to delve into the specific spiritual practices that amplify this connection with the divine feminine. These practices, both symbolic and meditative, help women to fully express their ability to balance feminine and masculine energies within themselves and around them. In addition, they provide means for both women and men to access and integrate this feminine spiritual dimension into their lives, promoting cosmic harmony.

The Lighting of Candles and the Inner Light

One of the most recognized spiritual practices in the Kabbalistic tradition is the lighting of Shabbat candles, a deeply meaningful ceremony that not only marks the beginning of the sacred day of rest but also symbolizes the act of bringing spiritual light into the world. In Kabbalistic mysticism, the woman who lights the candles is, in fact, playing a role as a mediator of divine light, inviting the presence of the Shechinah into her home and into the world. The candles represent the fusion of feminine and masculine energies, which unite to create harmony in the home and in the universe.

During the lighting, the woman covers her eyes while making the blessing, in a gesture that symbolizes the containment of light before its revelation. This practice is a metaphor for the Kabbalistic concept of Tzimtzum, in which God withdraws part of His infinite light so that the material world can exist. Similarly, the woman who covers her eyes is temporarily concealing the physical light to allow the spiritual light to flow and illuminate both the physical and spiritual space.

The act of lighting the candles also represents the creation of a space of peace and holiness. On the spiritual level, this is seen as a way of strengthening the woman's connection with the Sefirah of Binah, which represents understanding and wisdom. Meditation on the light of the candles can help women cultivate a deeper awareness of the divinity and their own role as guardians of spiritual light in the world.

Mikveh: Feminine Purification

Another central spiritual practice for women in Kabbalah is immersion in the Mikveh, the ritual bath of purification. This practice, which is related to the laws of family purity in Judaism, has deep mystical roots in the Kabbalistic tradition, especially with regard to renewal and spiritual transformation. Immersion in the Mikveh is seen as an act of purification and reconnection with the divine, symbolizing the return to the primordial source of creation.

In Kabbalah, the Mikveh is compared to the maternal womb, representing spiritual renewal and rebirth. Upon emerging from the water, the woman is seen as being recreated, renewed both physically and spiritually. The water of the Mikveh, according to Kabbalah, contains a purifying spiritual energy that cleanses not only the body but also the spirit, allowing the woman to reconnect with her divine essence.

This practice is also deeply connected to the cycle of the moon and the feminine energies associated with fertility and creation. The moon, a traditional symbol of the feminine, is associated with the menstrual cycle and cyclical renewal, reflecting the very natural processes of life. Immersion in the Mikveh, especially after the menstrual cycle, is seen as an act of harmonization with these natural energies, allowing the woman to align herself with the cosmic rhythms of creation and rebirth.

In the Kabbalistic tradition, meditation is a powerful tool for accessing and balancing spiritual energies. With regard to feminine energies, a common practice involves meditating on the Sefirot that are traditionally associated with the feminine, such as Binah (understanding), Malkhut (kingdom), and Chesed (kindness).

Binah, as we saw earlier, is associated with deep understanding and spiritual gestation. By meditating on this Sefirah, women can connect with their ability to create, nurture, and manifest both on the spiritual and physical levels. This meditation may involve visualizing a soft blue light, representing the flow of divine understanding that descends upon the meditator, providing wisdom and clarity.

Malkhut represents the physical realm, the lowest Sefirah on the Tree of Life, which receives and manifests all the energies of the higher Sefirot. It is often associated with the Shechinah and, therefore, with the divine presence in the material world. Meditating on Malkhut can help women connect with their role as manifestors of the divine presence on earth, especially in the realm of home and community. The visualization of a golden or silver light can help attract and amplify this energy of manifestation and protection.

Chesed, the Sefirah of kindness and compassion, is another powerful feminine force. It is associated with unconditional love and the act of giving. Meditation on Chesed involves cultivating feelings of kindness and compassion not only for others but also for oneself. Visualizing a flow of radiant white light can help awaken these qualities in the heart.

These meditations are not restricted to women only. Men can also practice them to attune themselves to the feminine energies within themselves, balancing the masculine and feminine in their own spiritual life.

Inner Balance: Integrating the Feminine and the Masculine

Although Kabbalah recognizes and honors the distinct nature of masculine and feminine energies, there is a continuous emphasis on the need for balance between them. Each person, regardless of gender, possesses within themselves masculine and feminine aspects that need to be harmonized to achieve spiritual wholeness.

For women, this balance may mean integrating the strength and discernment typical of masculine energies with the compassion and understanding of feminine energies. Meditations that involve the masculine Sefirot, such as Gevurah (strength) and Tiferet (beauty), can help in this process of harmonization. Similarly, men are encouraged to meditate on the feminine Sefirot to develop greater spiritual sensitivity and a deeper connection with the divine presence.

In Kabbalistic mysticism, the concept of co-creation is central. Just as the divine creates the universe continuously, human beings are seen as partners in this process of creation. Women, in particular, are considered co-creators on a deep level, not only in the physical sense but also in the spiritual sense. Their ability to generate and nurture life is mirrored in their ability to co-create with the divine through their actions, thoughts, and words.

This co-creation can be manifested in various ways: in caring for others, in the spiritual education of children, in creating a harmonious home, and in contributions to the community. Kabbalistic spiritual practice invites women to be conscious of their role as creators and to use their intuition, compassion, and strength to shape the world around them according to divine principles.

Although many of the spiritual practices of Kabbalah are specific to women, it is important to note that they can also be performed in a shared way, by both men and women, with the aim of promoting greater balance and harmony between masculine and feminine energies.

Joint meditation exercises, where the couple or community members meditate on the energies of the feminine and masculine Sefirot, can promote a deeper understanding of the interdependence between these forces. The recognition that both the feminine and the masculine are necessary for spiritual creation and for cosmic balance is a central principle in Kabbalah, and practices that emphasize this interconnection are powerful.

The role of women in Kabbalah is vast and multifaceted, involving both the recognition of their natural connection with divine feminine energies and the practice of rituals and meditations that amplify this connection. By cultivating their relationship with the Shechinah and the feminine Sefirot, women not only strengthen their own spiritual journey but also contribute to balance and harmony in the world around them.

Thus, Kabbalistic practice not only recognizes but celebrates the importance of the feminine as a creative, intuitive, and protective force. Whether through the traditions of Shabbat, immersion in the Mikveh, or meditations on the Sefirot, women are seen as a central figure in the continuity and manifestation of divine light in the world.

Chapter 21
The Zohar
The Book of Splendor

The Zohar, the Book of Splendor, is one of the central works of Kabbalah and Jewish mysticism. Written in Aramaic and organized as an esoteric commentary on the Torah, the Zohar presents a profound vision of the mysteries of creation, the human soul, and the interactions between the spiritual and material worlds. It is both a source of wisdom and a spiritual guide for those seeking to understand the relationship between the divine and the physical world.

The exact origin of the Zohar is a subject of discussion among scholars. Traditionally, it is believed to have been revealed by the sage Rabbi Shimon bar Yochai in the 2nd century CE, but there is a consensus that the Zohar, as we know it today, was compiled and disseminated by Rabbi Moses de Leon in the 13th century in Spain. Regardless of its origin, the Zohar contains profound teachings that transcend time and continue to inspire Kabbalah practitioners around the world.

The Zohar is a voluminous text, divided into different parts and treatises. It covers various themes ranging from mystical interpretations of the Torah to detailed descriptions of the spiritual worlds and the processes that govern creation. Although it is difficult to summarize the entire content of the Zohar in a few words, some of its central themes include:

Creation: The Zohar explores how the physical world was created from divine emanations, or Sefirot. It describes the process by which God, through different stages of concealment and revelation of His light, gave rise to the universe. The concept of Ein Sof, the Infinite Light that precedes all creation, is one of the foundations of these teachings.

The Tree of Life: One of the central symbols of the Zohar is the Tree of Life, a representation of the ten Sefirot. The Zohar discusses how these Sefirot interact with each other, forming a network of forces that govern both the spiritual and material worlds. Each Sefirah is associated with a specific aspect of the divine manifestation, and the study of the Zohar helps to unravel how these emanations work in harmony.

Man and the Soul: The Zohar offers a detailed view of the human soul, explaining how it is composed of different levels (such as Nefesh, Ruach, and Neshamah). It also describes the soul's journey through reincarnations and its connection to the universe. The idea that the human soul reflects the macrocosm is central to the Zohar, suggesting that each person has the potential to participate in the process of divine creation.

Duality and Unity: The Zohar often explores the tension between the opposing forces of light and darkness, good and evil, masculine and feminine. These forces, although seemingly antagonistic, are necessary to maintain the balance of creation. The Zohar teaches that by balancing these energies within oneself, the human being can align with the divine unity and achieve a higher spiritual harmony.

The Shechinah and Redemption: The Shechinah, the feminine divine presence, occupies a central place in the Zohar. She is seen as the force that resides in the material world, but also as an entity that seeks to reunite with her masculine aspect, represented by the higher Sefirot. The Zohar speaks of the need to correct the separation between these forces as a crucial step for the redemption of the world and the restoration of cosmic harmony.

Studying the Zohar requires not only a deep knowledge of the Torah and Kabbalah but also a spiritual willingness to contemplate its hidden meanings. The Zohar is not a text that can be read linearly or superficially. On the contrary, it was designed to be studied repeatedly, with new layers of meaning being revealed with each reading. Therefore, many Kabbalistic schools recommend that the study of the Zohar be accompanied by a master or spiritual guide, someone who has the necessary experience to help interpret its passages.

The Zohar uses a rich symbolic language, often full of metaphors and allegories that, at first glance, may seem obscure. This is because the Zohar was written to hide its secrets from the uninitiated, reserving its revelations for those who are ready to receive them. Many of its texts were organized in a way to stimulate deep meditation, guiding the student on an inner journey.

One of the most powerful techniques for studying the Zohar is meditation on its words. Many Kabbalists believe that simply reading or reciting the texts of the Zohar has a spiritual effect, even if the literal meaning is not completely understood. The vibration of the Aramaic and Hebrew words, according to these teachings, has the power to influence spiritual energies, creating a direct connection with the higher worlds.

The Impact of the Zohar on Kabbalah and Jewish Spirituality

The Zohar played a crucial role in the development of Kabbalah and profoundly shaped Jewish mysticism. It offered Kabbalah practitioners a complex framework for understanding creation and its relationship with God, but also provided a spiritual path that emphasizes the active role of the human being in the correction of the world, Tikun Olam.

Over the centuries, the Zohar has inspired many important figures in the history of Kabbalah, such as Rabbi Isaac Luria, also known as the Ari. Lurianic interpretations of the Zohar gave rise to Lurianic Kabbalah, a school of thought that further expanded the concepts presented in the Zohar, especially with regard to the role of man in the process of repairing the cosmos.

Furthermore, the Zohar had a profound impact on Hasidic Judaism, which emerged in Eastern Europe in the 18th century. Hasidic masters, such as the Baal Shem Tov, used the Zohar to teach that God is present in all aspects of everyday life, and that service to God is not restricted to moments of prayer or study, but must manifest in every action.

Today, the Zohar continues to be studied by millions of people around the world. The increased interest in spirituality and mysticism in recent decades has led many people, including those outside of Judaism, to explore the teachings of the Zohar as a source of spiritual wisdom and self-knowledge.

Study groups and academies dedicated to Kabbalah promote the reading and interpretation of the Zohar, both in Hebrew and in translations into other languages, allowing the knowledge contained in this sacred text to be more accessible than ever. However, many traditional Kabbalists still maintain that the Zohar should be studied with reverence and care, within the broader context of the Kabbalistic tradition.

The Zohar is an extraordinary work, a true jewel of mystical thought that transcends the barriers of time and culture. It offers a unique and transformative vision of the relationship between God, creation, and the human soul. For those seeking to explore the mysteries of existence and the depths of the spiritual, the Zohar is both a challenge and a treasure, revealing, layer by layer, the secrets of the universe.

By studying the Zohar, the reader is invited to embark on a spiritual journey that not only illuminates the path of the soul but also reveals the hidden dimensions of reality, opening a door to the true understanding of the divine and our place within creation.

Studying the Zohar requires more than just intellectual understanding; it also requires a deep spiritual commitment. The Zohar's approach is multidimensional, and the study of its texts involves opening the mind and heart to grasp its revelations. Kabbalistic tradition teaches that there are specific ways to access the secrets of the Zohar, each designed to guide the student towards spiritual enlightenment and communion with the divine.

Meditative Reading of the Zohar

One of the first steps to studying the Zohar in a practical way is to learn how to perform meditative reading, a method that combines the recitation of the texts with spiritual concentration. This practice involves not only reading the words but allowing them to penetrate the mind and soul, activating deep spiritual energies.

Kabbalists suggest that reading the Zohar can be done aloud, with careful intonation, paying attention to the sonority of the Aramaic words. The language of the Zohar carries, in itself, a mystical power; the words, even when not fully understood, have the ability to elevate consciousness. Recitation is accompanied by an intention (kavanah), a direction of the mind to connect with the divine light.

The meditative practice does not require the literal understanding of each passage, but rather immersion in the spiritual vibration that the texts provide. Some sections are studied for their direct effect on the reader's state of mind, while others, more complex, require the guidance of an experienced master. Students are encouraged to read the Zohar in moments of silence or after prayer, allowing its wisdom to permeate their reflections.

Studying the Zohar in a group is an important tradition in Kabbalistic mysticism. Gathering with other students creates a spiritual atmosphere that facilitates the opening of channels of deep understanding. In Kabbalistic study circles, reading together potentiates the spiritual energy of the Zohar, helping each individual to access its revelations more effectively.

During the meetings, each participant can share insights, experiences, and questions, promoting an environment of collective learning. This is in accordance with the idea that the Zohar, being a mystical work, was designed to be explored in a communal way, allowing different perspectives and levels of understanding to contribute to the construction of a more complete vision.

In addition, group study sessions often include discussions on how to apply the Kabbalistic principles learned in the readings to practical life. Since the Zohar deals with themes such as personal correction and the elevation of the soul, interactions between students often bring practical insights on how to transform these lessons into daily actions.

Some parts of the Zohar are particularly powerful for meditation and spiritual practices focused on healing, protection, or elevation of the soul. Below are some of the sections recommended for meditative study, along with their respective applications.

Introduction to the Zohar (Hakdamat Zohar) – This initial section offers an overview of the structure of the spiritual universe and the energies that shape the world. Meditation on this text is indicated for those seeking a broad view of the purpose of creation and their own role in the spiritual journey.

The Idra Rabba – One of the most profound and esoteric texts of the Zohar, it describes divine revelation in a context of intense spirituality. The study of the Idra Rabba is suggested for those who already have a certain foundation of Kabbalistic study and are ready to penetrate deeper mysteries about creation and the manifestation of divine light.

The Idra Zuta – This text focuses on the mystery of death and redemption, exploring the soul's transition from the physical to the spiritual world. Meditating on this section can bring a greater understanding of impermanence and the process of spiritual ascension after death.

The Tikunim – Meditation on the Tikunim, or corrections, described in the Zohar, is a powerful practice for those seeking personal and spiritual transformation. These sections deal with the need to correct imbalances in the Sefirot and align with divine harmony.

The Song of Songs in the Zohar – The Zohar offers a mystical interpretation of this biblical text, revealing the secrets of the union between the soul and God. Meditating on the Song of Songs in the context of the Zohar is a spiritual practice for those who wish to deepen their connection with the divine through love and devotion.

Kavanah, or intention, is one of the most essential aspects when studying and practicing the Zohar. It refers to the quality of attention and spiritual purpose that the practitioner brings to the study. More than just a mental attitude, kavanah is a way of concentrating the mind and heart towards the desired spiritual goal.

When studying the Zohar, kavanah can vary according to the objective of the meditation. For example, if the practitioner seeks wisdom about the creation of the universe, kavanah can be directed towards the contemplation of the Ein Sof (the Infinite Light) and the emanations of the Sefirot. For those seeking healing or spiritual protection, kavanah can be adjusted to the reception of divine blessings that flow through the words of the Zohar.

It is said that without adequate kavanah, the study of the Zohar loses part of its spiritual effectiveness. Therefore, practitioners are encouraged to align their thoughts and desires with the spiritual goals described in the texts, creating a bridge between the physical world and the higher spiritual realities.

Although it is possible to explore the Zohar individually, Kabbalistic tradition emphasizes the importance of studying with an experienced master. This is because the texts of the Zohar are complex and often enigmatic, containing layers of meaning that are not always evident to the novice reader.

The role of a teacher is to guide the student through the deeper interpretations of the text, helping to reveal the hidden secrets and to apply the teachings in a practical and relevant way. A Kabbalah master can provide detailed explanations of the most challenging passages, and also guide students in the practice of meditation and kavanah.

In ancient Kabbalistic traditions, the study of the Zohar was often reserved for more advanced students, those who had already mastered other areas of mystical knowledge. This ensured that practitioners were spiritually prepared to deal with the powerful and sometimes challenging insights contained in the Zohar. Although today the Zohar is more widely accessible, the value of a master's guidance remains invaluable.

In modern times, the Zohar continues to be a source of inspiration and transformation for those seeking a deep spiritual path. The study of the Zohar is not just an academic exercise; it is a commitment to spiritual evolution. As the world faces challenges of a material and spiritual nature, the Zohar offers answers that speak directly to the essence of human existence and the role of humanity in Tikun Olam, the correction of the world.

With the growth of global interest in spirituality and mysticism, the Zohar has been translated and disseminated in various languages, making its teachings accessible to people of different backgrounds. However, even with this wide dissemination, the teachings of the Zohar maintain their esoteric character, revealing themselves truly only to those who are prepared to receive them.

The practice of studying the Zohar is a continuous journey of self-discovery and spiritual elevation. The reader, by immersing themselves in the texts of the Zohar, not only acquires knowledge but also transforms. The wisdom contained in this book is a gateway to the mysteries of creation and the soul, an invitation to participate in the continuous process of correction and renewal that permeates all existence.

Chapter 22
Kabbalah and Material Prosperity

The relationship between spirituality and material prosperity is an ancient and fundamental question within Kabbalah. Contrary to what one might imagine, Kabbalah does not view the material world as something to be rejected or separated from the spiritual quest. On the contrary, it teaches that the balance between the material and the spiritual is essential for the fulfillment of life's purpose and the accomplishment of each human being's divine mission.

Kabbalah recognizes that the material world is an expression of divinity and, therefore, material prosperity is not only permitted but also encouraged, as long as it is aligned with elevated spiritual values. The challenge is not to possess material goods, but rather to ensure that these goods are in service of the spiritual purpose.

In the Kabbalistic view, the concept of prosperity is rooted in the idea that God created the world to be abundant and full. Material prosperity is a way of manifesting divine abundance in the physical world. However, this abundance should not be confused with the selfish accumulation of wealth. The purpose of prosperity, according to Kabbalah, is to allow people to fulfill their spiritual missions more effectively and contribute to Tikun Olam, the repair of the world.

Prosperity, then, is seen as a tool that can be used to build a more just and balanced world. When wealth is generated and used ethically and consciously, it becomes a blessing, helping to elevate the physical world to its spiritual potential. In this context, true success is not measured by the amount of material goods one possesses, but by the positive impact that these resources have on the individual's life and the community.

Kabbalah teaches that divine energies, manifested in the Sefirot, also play an important role in how material prosperity is understood and experienced. Each Sefirah, or divine emanation, carries a particular quality that can influence the way we interact with wealth and material resources.

Chessed (Kindness): The Sefirah of Chessed is associated with generosity and the abundant flow of blessings. It represents openness and the willingness to share, demonstrating that true prosperity involves giving to others and participating in the flow of divine abundance.

Gevurah (Strength): Gevurah, on the other hand, symbolizes restriction and self-control. It teaches us that material prosperity must be balanced with responsibility and discipline. The ability to manage material resources wisely is fundamental to ensure that wealth is not an obstacle to spiritual growth.

Tiferet (Beauty): Tiferet is the Sefirah that balances Chessed and Gevurah. It represents harmony and balance between giving and receiving. In the context of material prosperity, Tiferet reminds us that it is important to find a middle ground, where generosity is balanced by careful management of resources.

These three Sefirot—Chessed, Gevurah, and Tiferet—provide a solid foundation for the Kabbalistic understanding of prosperity. They teach us that wealth, when balanced by kindness, self-control, and harmony, can be a powerful tool for personal and social transformation.

Kabbalah emphasizes the role of free will in how we interact with the material world. We are constantly confronted with choices that involve how we deal with money and material goods. These choices reflect our level of spiritual awareness. Money, being a form of energy, can be channeled for good or for selfishness, and this choice belongs to each individual.

Free will is fundamental to the Kabbalistic understanding of prosperity. Wealth can be both a blessing and a curse, depending on how it is used. If someone seeks wealth exclusively for selfish reasons, the accumulation of material goods can become a spiritual prison. On the other hand, if prosperity is sought with the intention of promoting well-being and spiritual progress, it becomes a powerful force for good.

This distinction is vital, as it reflects Kabbalah's view that the purpose of life is not simply to accumulate wealth, but to use it in a way that contributes to the greater good. Free will gives us the power to choose what to do with the resources we receive, and it is this choice that defines our spiritual path.

Another central point in the Kabbalistic approach to prosperity is the idea that work is a form of spiritual expression. Work, in Kabbalah, is not just a way to make a living; it is an opportunity to participate in the ongoing act of creation. By working with integrity and a higher purpose, the individual aligns with the divine flow of creative energy.

The Zohar, one of the central texts of Kabbalah, teaches that each person's life force is channeled into the work they do. Therefore, work should not be seen as an obligation or a burden, but as a way to bring light into the world. When work is done with the correct intention—for the benefit of the soul and the world—it transforms into a spiritual practice in itself.

The Kabbalistic concept of Avodah, which means both "work" and "service," reflects this idea. Work is a form of serving God, contributing to the elevation of the material world. This includes both professional work and the inner work of self-improvement and personal correction.

One of the most important principles of Kabbalah in relation to prosperity is the concept of Tzedakah, which means charity but also justice. In the Kabbalistic view, wealth brings with it the responsibility to share and help those in need. The act of giving to others is not just a moral choice, but a fundamental spiritual practice.

Tzedakah is seen as a powerful means of elevating the soul and transforming material energy into spirituality. By giving to others, the individual participates in the divine flow of blessings, opening themselves to receive more in return. This should not be seen as a materialistic exchange, but as a spiritual reciprocity: by sharing prosperity, the individual aligns with the universal principle that abundance should circulate.

Furthermore, the practice of Tzedakah is one of the most direct methods to correct the selfish consciousness that can accompany the accumulation of wealth. By giving, the individual detaches from materialism and reinforces the idea that true prosperity is measured by the positive impact one has on the world.

Kabbalah teaches that the true secret of material prosperity lies in detachment. Paradoxically, the less we are attached to material wealth, the more open we are to receiving the blessings of divine abundance. Excessive attachment to material goods can create spiritual blockages, distancing the person from the true source of abundance, which is divine light.

Detachment, in Kabbalah, does not mean renouncing material goods, but rather understanding that they are temporary and that their real value lies in how they are used to promote good. Material prosperity should be seen as a tool for spiritual fulfillment, and not as an end in itself. By practicing detachment, the individual opens themselves to the flow of abundance and learns to live in harmony with the spiritual laws of the universe.

Material prosperity, according to Kabbalah, is not only about physical wealth, but about how that wealth is obtained, managed, and used. It is a manifestation of the balance between the spiritual and the material, a reflection of free will, and an opportunity to practice divine service through work and charity. The true purpose of wealth, in Kabbalah, is to contribute to the greater good, promoting Tikun Olam and aligning with divine light.

In the second part of the discussion on material prosperity within Kabbalah, it is essential to delve into how these teachings can be applied in the practical life of the individual. What Kabbalah offers is not just a philosophical or theological vision, but a set of practical guidelines for humans to harmonize their relationship with wealth and use it as a tool for spiritual growth.

The concept of Kavanah, or intention, is central to all Kabbalistic practices, and the question of material prosperity is no different. In Kabbalah, the intention with which an act is performed is as important as the act itself. When a person seeks material prosperity, the question they must ask themselves is: "Why am I seeking this wealth? How will it help me serve a greater purpose?"

To align with spiritual prosperity, it is important to set a clear and elevated intention for the use of material resources. When working, undertaking, or seeking financial opportunities, the Kavanah should be not only for personal benefit, but how this prosperity can be used for the greater good. Kabbalah teaches that when one has an intention to serve the universe and contribute to Tikun Olam, the flow of financial blessings tends to open up in a more natural and abundant way.

Kabbalah offers meditative practices that can help align the mind with divine abundance and remove the blocks that impede the flow of prosperity. One of these meditations involves the use of the Sefirot, the divine emanations that serve as channels of energy between the spiritual and material worlds. Meditating on the Sefirot can help cultivate a mindset of abundance, focusing on balance and harmony.

One of the most powerful meditations for material prosperity involves the Sefirah of Tiferet, which represents harmony and balance between giving and receiving. To practice this meditation, the reader can imagine the energy of Tiferet as a golden light that descends from the higher plane to the heart, radiating harmony between their material needs and their spiritual purpose. While breathing deeply, visualize this light flowing to all areas of your life that are related to prosperity—work, finances, personal projects. The intention here is to cultivate an awareness that prosperity is not something separate from the spiritual, but a harmonious expression of the same divine flow.

This visualization practice can be accompanied by a simple Kabbalistic prayer: "May my prosperity be a reflection of the harmony between my spirit and my actions in the world." Repeated regularly, this meditation helps align consciousness with the higher purpose of abundance.

Work is another fundamental aspect in the manifestation of material prosperity. As previously discussed, Kabbalah sees work as a form of Avodah, or divine service. To transform work into a spiritual practice, it is crucial to cultivate a mindset of purpose and presence.

Kabbalistic practice encourages that, before starting any work, the individual take a brief pause to connect with the spiritual intention of what they are about to accomplish. This can be done with a silent prayer or reflection, asking that the work to be done bring benefits not only to the worker, but to those who will be impacted by the results of that work. By adopting this daily practice, the reader can begin to transform their work routine into a spiritually meaningful activity, and not just a means to achieve wealth.

Kabbalah teaches that material wealth should be used consciously and ethically. One of the fundamental practices to ensure that prosperity is used correctly is tithing, or Maasser. In the Kabbalistic tradition, Maasser is the practice of donating a percentage of one's earnings (usually 10%) to charitable causes or to help the less fortunate.

This practice is not only an act of charity, but also a way to purify material wealth. Money, being a form of energy, can carry negative energies, especially when obtained in unbalanced ways. By giving a portion of this wealth for the good of others, the person "purifies" the remainder, making it more likely to bring blessings and abundance. The practice of Maasser also reinforces detachment and the understanding that prosperity is not an end in itself, but a tool to serve others.

Furthermore, the act of giving helps break the cycle of attachment to materialism, creating a space for more blessings to flow. Kabbalah teaches that by giving generously, the person opens themselves to receive more, as they align with the divine flow of abundance.

Another important aspect in the pursuit of material prosperity is spiritual protection. Often, when seeking material success, people can expose themselves to negative influences—both external and internal, such as pride, greed, and the temptation to harm others to achieve their goals.

Kabbalah offers several practices to protect the spirit during this journey. One of them is the use of Divine Names in meditation and prayer. For example, the Tetragrammaton YHVH, which represents the essence of the divine, can be chanted or visualized in moments of doubt or temptation. Visualizing the divine name enveloping the body in light, protecting it from negative energies and keeping the mind clear and focused, is a simple but powerful practice.

Additionally, the practice of Hakarat HaTov—the recognition of goodness—is a way to protect the soul against the dangers of dissatisfaction and insatiable desire. By recognizing and giving thanks for the blessings already received, the individual remains anchored in the present, avoiding the trap of always seeking more without purpose. Gratitude activates positive energy and protects against the destructive aspects of greed and materialism.

Sometimes, despite the best intentions, people may feel that there are blocks in their flow of prosperity. Kabbalah recognizes that the flow of energy can be interrupted by spiritual and emotional blockages, such as limiting beliefs about money, fear of scarcity, or guilt regarding wealth.

A practical way to deal with these blockages is the practice of Heshbon HaNefesh, the spiritual accounting. This involves a regular self-assessment, where the individual reflects on their attitudes towards prosperity, identifying fears, limiting beliefs, or self-sabotaging behaviors. Questions like "Am I using my resources in a balanced way?", "Am I afraid of not having enough?", or "How can I use my wealth to serve the world?" are essential to realign the energy flow.

After identifying the blockages, purification practices such as the use of the Mikveh, the Kabbalistic ritual bath, can be incorporated to cleanse stagnant energy and reopen the channels of abundance. These practices reinforce the idea that prosperity is a reflection of the internal state, and that cleansing and aligning the soul is fundamental to attracting material prosperity.

Finally, prayer plays a vital role in the manifestation of material prosperity. In Kabbalah, specific prayers, such as those found in the Book of Psalms, are used to invoke abundance and divine protection over finances. One of the Psalms most used for this purpose is Psalm 23, which speaks of trust in divine providence: "The Lord is my shepherd; I shall not want."

The daily practice of prayers of gratitude and requests for divine guidance on finances helps keep the mind connected with the higher purpose of prosperity, preventing the pursuit of wealth from becoming a trap for the ego. These prayers can be done in moments of financial uncertainty, or simply as a way to maintain constant gratitude for the prosperity already achieved.

Material prosperity, when aligned with spirituality, becomes a transformative force, both for the individual and for the world around them. Kabbalah teaches us that true wealth is not only in the possession of material goods, but in the wise and ethical use of these resources to serve a greater purpose. By applying Kabbalistic practices—from meditations to tithing, through gratitude and prayer—the reader can transform their relationship with prosperity, attracting it in a balanced and harmonious way.

Chapter 23
The 72 Names of God

In Kabbalah, the 72 Names of God form a sacred sequence of letters, each containing powerful spiritual energies that can be accessed for transformation, protection, and elevation. These Names are not names in the traditional sense, but combinations of three Hebrew letters extracted from a specific passage in the Torah. They represent different aspects of the divinity, and each Name reflects a specific energy that can be invoked through meditations, prayers, and Kabbalistic practices.

The origin of the 72 Names of God dates back to an episode in the Torah, when Moses and the people of Israel were standing before the Red Sea. Kabbalistic tradition teaches that three consecutive verses from the Book of Exodus (14:19-21), each composed of 72 letters, provide the code for these sacred names. When arranged in combinations of three letters, these sequences form the 72 expressions of divine power, which can be used to access different types of spiritual energy.

The 72 Names of God should not be seen merely as mystical words or abstract concepts. Each of these combinations represents a key to accessing higher spiritual realities and energies that can directly influence the physical world and the human soul. Kabbalists teach that behind each Name, there is a portal that connects the seeker to the divine essence, allowing the invocation of blessings, protection, and healing.

Each of the 72 combinations is composed of three Hebrew letters that correspond to a specific aspect of creation and divinity. These names are used in Kabbalistic spiritual practices as a way to channel these energies in a practical and direct way. Different names can be used for different purposes, such as physical healing, protection against negative influences, increasing spiritual intuition, or overcoming challenges.

The most powerful aspect of the 72 Names of God is their ability to connect the practitioner directly with the pure energy of creation. By meditating on these combinations, the reader can unlock new realities and internal transformations that positively impact their external environment.

The practice of the 72 Names of God involves meditation and visualization. The practitioner focuses on the sequence of Hebrew letters, often imagining them in their mind or visualizing them as if they were shining with divine light. The goal is to connect with the energy associated with the specific name, allowing its force to enter the practitioner's life.

Kabbalists teach that each of the 72 Names acts as a kind of "spiritual tool" that can be used to achieve a particular goal. These goals can range from spiritual strengthening, protection against negative energies, to physical and emotional healing.

For example, the Name Aleph-Lamed-Dalet (ALD) is associated with protection against evil and negative energies. Visualizing these three letters while meditating can help create a protective shield around the person, warding off destructive influences. On the other hand, the Name Mem-He-Shin (MHS) is used for healing and restoration. By focusing on this combination during meditation, the practitioner can channel healing energy to themselves or to others.

The power of the 72 Names of God can be applied in various areas of life. From practical matters, such as making important decisions, to spiritual dilemmas, the practice with these names offers a direct way to access spiritual support. Each Name corresponds to a specific need or challenge and can be used to address various situations. Here are some ways to apply the 72 Names in everyday life:

Spiritual Protection: Many of the Names are used to create a protective barrier against negative forces. Meditating with the protective Names before an important meeting or in moments of uncertainty can bring more clarity and security. The Name Samech-Aleph-Lamed (SAL) is particularly effective for protection against negativity and envy.

Healing: Names like Mem-He-Shin (MHS) are used in healing practices. These meditations can be directed to a specific part of the body or to the energy field as a whole, helping to restore physical and emotional balance. Healing is not limited to the physical body; it can be applied to emotional and spiritual healing, helping to release blockages or traumas.

Overcoming Challenges: When facing difficulties, the Name Aleph-Kaf-Aleph (AKA) can be invoked to overcome obstacles and find strength in times of adversity. Visualizing this Name during meditation helps the practitioner access courage and resilience.

Wisdom and Spiritual Clarity: For those seeking answers or greater spiritual understanding, the Name Yod-Lamed-Yod (YLY) is a valuable tool. It helps to open the mind to wisdom and clarity in situations that seem confusing or obscure.

Emotional Balance: If the practitioner feels that their emotions are unbalanced or that they are stuck in cycles of anxiety or stress, the Name Hey-Hey-Ayin (HHA) can be useful. This Name promotes serenity and harmony, helping to align emotions with the soul.

Visualizing the 72 Names of God during meditation is a fundamental technique in Kabbalah. Visualization involves concentrating on the Hebrew letters and seeing them not only as static symbols, but as portals of living light, radiating divine energy. This practice should be accompanied by deep breaths and a clear intention. Intention is what directs the energy of the Names, allowing them to work effectively in the practitioner's life.

To begin a meditation with the 72 Names, the reader can follow these steps:

Sit in a quiet place and close your eyes.

Breathe deeply a few times, calming your mind and body.

Visualize the three letters of the chosen Name as if they were written in golden or white light in front of you.

Concentrate on the energy associated with these letters. Imagine that the light of the letters enters your body, filling it with divine energy.

Maintain focus on this Name for a few minutes, mentally repeating or visualizing the letters while breathing deeply.

When finished, give thanks for any insights or energy received.

Connection with the Divine Through the Names

The 72 Names of God also serve as a means to deepen the connection with the divine. Each Name is like a "thread" that connects us directly to the Source of Creation. When we meditate on these Names, we are activating the connection between our soul and the higher spiritual plane. It is a practice that goes beyond mere recitation or visualization — it is a form of spiritual elevation, in which we become aware of our own divinity and the creative power that dwells within us.

Kabbalists teach that, by using the 72 Names of God, we approach the original state of unity with the Creator. Each practice takes us one step closer to the state of Tiferet — the balance and harmony between body, mind, and spirit.

The 72 Names of God are one of the deepest secrets of Kabbalah, providing the practitioner with direct access to powerful spiritual energies that can be used for personal transformation, protection, and healing. These Names are not just letters, but keys to accessing spiritual portals that connect us to the Source. By integrating these Names into daily practices, the reader can experience a profound change in the way they interact with the world and with their own spirit. The next part of this study will delve into the specific practices of meditation and activation of the Names, allowing the reader to apply these teachings in their life even more effectively.

Now that the introduction to the 72 Names of God has been made and their fundamental meanings have been presented, it is time to delve into the practical use of these Names. Kabbalah teaches that the true power of the 72 Names is accessed through specific spiritual practices. These exercises involve meditation, repetition, and visualization of the Names, always with the clear intention of bringing their energies into different areas of life.

One of the most effective ways to connect with the 72 Names of God is through meditation. Meditative practice allows the practitioner to align their consciousness with the energies of the Names and absorb their spiritual vibrations. As each Name is a combination of three Hebrew letters, meditation involves concentrating deeply on these letters and allowing their energies to be integrated into the body, mind, and spirit.

A basic meditation can be done as follows:

Choose a Name: Determine which Name you want to work with, according to your spiritual need at the moment. It can be for protection, healing, mental clarity, or any other purpose you need.

Find a quiet place: Sit in a calm place free from distractions. An upright posture helps keep the mind alert and the body relaxed.

Breathe deeply: Start with a few deep breaths. This helps calm the mind and prepare the body for meditation. As you exhale, imagine releasing any tensions or concerns.

Visualize the Name: Imagine the three Hebrew letters of the Name floating in front of you. They can appear shining in white, golden, or blue light, depending on how you feel most connected. Focus your attention completely on these letters.

Intention and invocation: While visualizing the Name, visualize the intention for which you are meditating. For example, if you are seeking healing, imagine that the healing energy of the letters is being absorbed by your body, purifying and restoring your balance.

Repeat the Name: Silently or whispering, repeat the Name several times, synchronizing your breath with the letters. This helps amplify the connection and energize your spiritual field.

Closing: After a few minutes, take another deep breath and let the image of the letters slowly fade away. Give thanks for the energy and wisdom received during the practice.

This simple meditation can be performed daily or whenever the practitioner feels the need to access the energies of the Names.

The power of the 72 Names of God manifests in various areas of life, and each Name has a specific application. Below, we will see how to use some of these Names in practical everyday situations:

Healing: The Name Mem-He-Shin (MHS) is widely used for healing, whether physical or emotional. When meditating on this Name, visualize the three letters shining over the area that needs healing, whether it is a specific part of the body or an emotional aspect that is out of balance. The light emanating from the letters fills your body with healing energy, restoring inner harmony.

Protection: To protect yourself from negative energies or external influences, the Name Samech-Aleph-Lamed (SAL) is a powerful spiritual tool. This Name creates a protective energy field around you, like an invisible shield that prevents any negativity from penetrating your aura. When visualizing it, imagine a sphere of light around you, filled with the protective energy emanating from the letters.

Overcoming Challenges: When life presents obstacles that seem insurmountable, the Name Aleph-Kaf-Aleph (AKA) can provide the spiritual strength needed to overcome them. Meditate on this Name while visualizing the challenges you are facing. The letters provide the energy of persistence and courage, allowing you to see new paths or solutions that previously seemed invisible.

Wisdom and Spiritual Clarity: For those seeking divine guidance or greater clarity in their decisions, the Name Yod-Lamed-Yod (YLY) is used to open channels of spiritual wisdom. Visualize this Name while reflecting on a situation where you need guidance. It can bring insights and allow you to see the situation from a higher and more enlightened perspective.

Increased Intuition: The Name Nun-Yod-Tav (NYT) is used to increase intuition and strengthen the connection with your inner self. This Name helps to open the channels of spiritual perception, allowing you to hear the "inner voice" more clearly and make intuitive decisions that are aligned with your higher purpose.

In addition to meditation, the 72 Names of God are also used in Kabbalistic prayers and mantras. The repetition of these Names, along with a specific prayer or mantra, can amplify the power of the invocation. When praying with the Names, it is important to focus on the intention and meaning behind each of the letters.

A practical example is the repetition of the Name Aleph-Lamed-Dalet (ALD) to ward off evil. This prayer can be used in moments of fear, uncertainty, or when one feels the presence of negative forces around. The repetition of the Name can be done aloud or mentally, always with the visualization of the letters while repeating the mantra. The prayer can be simple, such as:

"May the sacred Name Aleph-Lamed-Dalet protect me and keep me safe, warding off any evil or negative influence that may be present around me."

For more experienced practitioners, an advanced visualization technique with the 72 Names involves creating an energy field around the entire body. This practice helps to fully integrate the energy of the Names into the practitioner's auric field, strengthening their spiritual connection and expanding their field of protection.

Here is an advanced visualization practice:

Creation of the Circle of Light: Imagine that you are sitting inside a circle of golden light. This circle is made of the energies of the 72 Names. Each of the letters shines brightly, forming a barrier of light around you.

Visualization of the Body of Light: As you continue to visualize the circle of light, begin to see your body filling with this divine light. Each cell of your body begins to shine with the energy of the 72 Names.

Expansion of Energy: Imagine now that the light of the Names begins to expand beyond your body, reaching everything around you — the space you are in, the people around you, and even the external environment. This field of light acts as a blessing, radiating energy of healing, protection, and harmony to all beings.

Integration and Gratitude: At the end of the visualization, feel the light begin to return to within you, integrating completely into your soul. Give thanks for this spiritual experience and for the power of the Names in your life.

As in all spiritual practices, consistency is key. The energy of the 72 Names of God is most effective when invoked regularly. One can choose a Name to work with daily, dedicating time to meditation and repetition of that Name throughout the day. Regularity strengthens the connection with the divine energies and increases the practitioner's ability to access their blessings and powers.

Whether in the search for healing, protection, wisdom, or personal transformation, the 72 Names of God offer a powerful way to access the divine. By using them with respect and clear intention, the practitioner begins to transform their reality from the inside out, experiencing a life more aligned with the light and wisdom of creation.

The 72 Names of God are one of the most profound and transformative tools of Kabbalah. Not only do they offer a way to connect directly with elevated spiritual energies, but they also allow the practitioner to shape their life in alignment with divine purpose. By mastering the practices of meditation, visualization, and prayer with the Names, the reader will be able to access an inexhaustible source of wisdom, healing, and protection.

Chapter 24
Kabbalah and the Future

Kabbalah, as a spiritual tradition that seeks a deep understanding of the mysteries of the universe, also offers insights into the future of humanity and global spiritual evolution. Through the Kabbalistic perspective, the future is not seen as something fixed and predestined, but as a field of possibilities influenced by individual and collective actions. Kabbalah suggests that the destiny of humanity is intrinsically linked to the process of spiritual correction known as Tikkun Olam, which means "repairing the world." This central concept in Kabbalah asserts that each human being plays a role in restoring cosmic harmony, raising consciousness, and bringing light to the world.

One of the fundamental ideas about the future, as taught in Kabbalah, is that the world is in a state of constant transition between darkness and light, chaos and order, fragmentation and unity. This cycle reflects the struggle between the opposing forces that shape creation, something that has already been discussed in the chapter on duality in the Kabbalistic system. However, the ultimate goal of humanity, according to Kabbalistic teachings, is to achieve a state of equilibrium, where chaos and darkness are overcome by light and divine harmony.

Kabbalah brings forth a concept of "final days" or "end of times," which does not necessarily refer to an apocalypse or destruction, but rather to a profound spiritual transformation. In the Zohar, the most important text of Kabbalah, there are passages that speak of the arrival of an era of great spiritual enlightenment, in which truth and divine knowledge will be fully revealed to humanity. This revelation will be the climax of millennia of spiritual search and correction, in which souls will finally achieve a state of unity with the Creator.

In the Kabbalistic view, time is not linear, but cyclical. This means that, instead of moving forward in a straight line towards a definitive end, history and time repeat themselves in cycles, each time bringing new levels of understanding and spiritual growth. The current cycle, according to some Kabbalists, is at a crucial moment, where humanity is about to take an evolutionary leap in terms of spiritual consciousness. This leap is described as the emergence of a new era of wisdom and enlightenment, where the separation between the divine and the human will finally be dissolved.

This future period is often associated with the concept of the "messianic era," a time when justice, peace, and harmony will prevail in the world. However, Kabbalah emphasizes that the Messiah, or the messianic era, does not depend solely on the coming of an individual or spiritual leader, but is the result of a collective effort by humanity to raise its consciousness and carry out Tikkun Olam. Each person who works to correct themselves and the world around them is contributing to the arrival of this new era.

Kabbalah sees global spiritual evolution as a gradual and continuous process, involving both humanity and the universe as a whole. The universe is seen as a living and interconnected organism, in which every human action, thought, and intention influences the whole. Spiritual correction, therefore, is not an isolated process, but involves the active participation of all souls, both incarnate and those who have already transcended.

As humanity advances on its spiritual journey, Kabbalah teaches that we will see a collective elevation of consciousness. The barriers that currently separate people—such as cultural, religious, and ideological differences—will begin to dissolve, and the perception that all human beings share a common divine essence will be more widely recognized. This state of unity, or *Achdut*, is one of the main goals of Kabbalah and Tikkun Olam.

However, this spiritual progress does not occur without challenges. Kabbalah states that spiritual darkness and the forces of chaos intensify as we approach great evolutionary leaps. These forces represent the uncorrected aspects of creation—parts of the world that have not yet been brought to light. Thus, humanity may face periods of great turbulence, both on a personal and global level, before the light prevails.

The 72 Names of God, presented earlier, play an important role in the process of spiritual evolution described by Kabbalah. These Names are powerful tools for accessing divine energies that can accelerate the process of correction both on a personal and global level. As humanity moves towards an era of spiritual enlightenment, the 72 Names will continue to be used by Kabbalistic practitioners to facilitate healing, protection, and transformation.

Each Name is a key that unlocks different aspects of spiritual reality. As more people connect with these energies and begin to use them consciously, the collective vibration of the planet rises. This not only benefits individuals, but also positively influences the environment around them, creating a ripple effect of light that can reach even those who are not directly engaged in spiritual practices.

An important aspect of the future in the Kabbalistic view is the role of free will. Kabbalah teaches that, although humanity's ultimate spiritual destiny is union with the Creator, the path to achieving this state depends on the choices we make throughout our lives. Free will is what allows us to actively participate in the process of Tikkun Olam and in the correction of ourselves and the world. Every choice we make has the potential to bring us closer to or further away from this ultimate goal.

The Zohar emphasizes that, as long as there is darkness and chaos in the world, human beings will continue to face moral and spiritual dilemmas. These choices are part of the process of growth and evolution, as it is through overcoming challenges and correcting our mistakes that we grow spiritually. Thus, the future of humanity, according to Kabbalah, is not a fixed destiny, but something that is being constantly shaped by the decisions we make individually and collectively.

Kabbalah not only offers us a vision of the future, but also calls us to action. It teaches that each person has the power to influence the future through their daily actions. The concept of Tikkun Olam reminds us that we are not passively at the mercy of global or cosmic events, but are active participants in the creation of our own destiny and the destiny of the world.

For Kabbalah, spiritual practices, such as meditation, the study of sacred texts, and the use of the 72 Names of God, are powerful tools to help create a future of light and harmony. In addition, acts of kindness, justice, and compassion are seen as tangible expressions of spiritual correction, contributing directly to the construction of a better world.

Individual action, when done with intention and awareness, reverberates throughout creation, influencing not only the present, but also future generations. Kabbalah reminds us that, by correcting ourselves and our immediate environment, we are, in fact, participating in the creation of a more enlightened future for all.

The future, according to Kabbalah, is a journey towards spiritual unity and global correction. Humanity is in a continuous process of spiritual evolution, where every action, choice, and intention influences the collective destiny. Although the path may be challenging, Kabbalah offers powerful tools—such as the 72 Names of God and the concept of Tikkun Olam—to help humanity overcome darkness and move towards the light.

Now that we understand the Kabbalistic view of the future of humanity and the concept of Tikkun Olam as a process of global and spiritual correction, it is time to focus on how each of us can actively participate in the creation of this future. Kabbalah does not see destiny as something passive or predefined; instead, it invites us to be co-creators, conscious participants in the process of spiritual evolution of the universe. The Kabbalistic tools we have studied so far offer a solid foundation to begin this journey.

Kabbalah teaches that the physical world is only a manifestation of higher spiritual realities. Every action, thought, and intention we have affects not only our personal world, but also the collective world. One of the central teachings of Kabbalah is the power of consciousness. Consciousness, when directed correctly, can transform both our internal and external reality. For Kabbalah, raising consciousness is the most direct path to bringing more light into the world and accelerating the process of Tikkun Olam.

When we speak of "raising consciousness," we refer to the ability to perceive the interconnectedness of all things. Kabbalah teaches us that all souls are connected, and that what affects one person or one part of creation affects the whole. Every thought of kindness, every intention to do good, generates waves of energy that influence the collective spiritual field. Likewise, every choice based on selfishness or separation negatively affects the spiritual balance of the world.

Therefore, Kabbalistic practice emphasizes the importance of self-observation and conscious intention in our actions. When we make a conscious choice to elevate our actions to the spiritual level—whether through acts of kindness, meditation, or study—we are directly contributing to the collective spiritual progress. This is what Kabbalah describes as "bringing light to the world." With each act of light, we help to dispel the shadows of spiritual darkness that still surround humanity.

There are several Kabbalistic spiritual practices that we can incorporate into our daily lives to actively participate in the process of Tikkun Olam. These practices not only help us to evolve spiritually, but also create a positive impact on the world around us. Below, we explore some of these practices and how to apply them.

As we saw earlier, the 72 Names of God are a powerful spiritual tool that can be used to access different levels of divine energy. Meditation with these Names allows the practitioner to connect directly with the creative source of the universe, promoting healing, protection, and spiritual transformation. Each Name is a key to opening spiritual portals that can bring more light and harmony to the world.

To meditate with the 72 Names, the practitioner must first choose a specific Name that represents the energy or purpose they wish to manifest—whether healing, wisdom, protection, or any other intention.

Then, they visualize the letters of the Name in their mind, meditating on its meaning and the energy it evokes. During this meditation, it is important to maintain a clear intention of how this energy will be used to bring light to the world.

This practice can be done daily or at specific moments of spiritual need. The impact of regular meditations with the 72 Names not only benefits the practitioner, but also emanates healing energies to the environment around them, contributing to global spiritual elevation.

Prayer, in Kabbalah, is much more than a simple repetition of words; it is a way of aligning human will with divine will. Conscious prayer is that which is done with a clear and focused intention, seeking not only personal benefits, but also collective well-being. When we pray, especially with the words of sacred texts or Psalms, we create a bridge between the physical and spiritual worlds, allowing divine energies to flow more freely.

Kabbalah suggests that when we pray for other people, for peace in the world, or for the correction of spiritual flaws, we are performing Tikkun Olam. This practice reinforces the Kabbalistic concept that individuality is connected with the collective, and that by correcting a part, we contribute to the correction of the whole.

In addition to meditative practices and prayers, Kabbalah places great emphasis on action in the material world as a form of spiritual transformation. Acts of kindness, or *Chessed*, are seen as a direct expression of the divine energy of love and mercy. Whenever we practice an act of generosity, helping another person, or contributing to the well-being of our environment, we are acting as channels for divine light.

These acts of kindness can be simple—such as offering help to someone in need or performing voluntary actions for a greater cause—but their spiritual impact is profound. Kabbalah teaches that each act of *Chessed* we perform generates light in the world, helping to balance energies and heal the spiritual darkness that still exists.

The continuous study of Kabbalistic teachings is also a way of participating in the process of spiritual correction. By dedicating ourselves to study, especially of texts like the Zohar and the Sefer Yetzirah, we are not only expanding our own spiritual understanding, but also contributing to the collective awakening. The wisdom contained in these texts teaches us about the spiritual laws that govern the universe, and how we can live in accordance with these laws to bring more light and balance to the world.

Kabbalah views study as a form of active meditation. When we study with intention and depth, we connect with the spiritual energies contained in the words and awaken higher parts of our own soul. The knowledge we acquire, in turn, can be applied in our daily lives, allowing us to act in a more conscious and spiritualized way.

One of the most powerful messages of Kabbalah about the future is the idea that the destiny of the world depends on collective effort. Each soul plays a unique role in the process of correction, and the more people consciously engage in this process, the faster the world reaches a state of harmony and peace.

Kabbalah teaches us that there is an interdependence between all souls. When one soul rises, it elevates others around it. This means that even small acts of kindness or moments of spiritual introspection can have much greater effects than we imagine. Likewise, when a person works to correct their spiritual flaws, they contribute to the correction of all humanity. This understanding gives us a new perspective on the importance of our daily actions, reinforcing the notion that every choice we make has profound spiritual repercussions.

The Kabbalistic view of the future is deeply optimistic. Although humanity faces spiritual and moral challenges, Kabbalah firmly believes that the ultimate destiny of the world is unity with the Creator. This unity does not mean uniformity, but a harmonious integration of the differences and uniqueness of each soul, where all parts of creation coexist in peace and balance.

The process of Tikkun Olam is the path to achieving this unity. Through spiritual practice, the elevation of consciousness, and acts of kindness, humanity gradually corrects the flaws that separated it from the divine source. Kabbalah sees this process as inevitable, although its acceleration depends on the choices we make as individuals and as a collective.

The future, as revealed by Kabbalah, is a collective journey towards spiritual enlightenment and the correction of the world. Each of us has the responsibility and the privilege of actively participating in this process, whether through meditative practices, acts of kindness, or spiritual study. Kabbalah offers us the tools and the map to realize this future, and it is up to each of us to decide how to use them.

As we move forward on this journey, it is essential to remember that the process of Tikkun Olam is a continuous path, where every step counts.

Chapter 25
Final Reflections
The Kabbalistic Journey

As we approach the end of this book, it is important to pause and reflect on the depth of the journey we have taken so far. From the first steps in understanding the fundamentals of Kabbalah to the more complex teachings on the interaction between the human and the divine, we have been invited to explore a spiritual path that, at its core, seeks not only to explain the universe but to profoundly transform our relationship with it.

Kabbalah is not just an esoteric theory; it is a living practice, a system of self-knowledge and spiritual elevation that encompasses all aspects of existence. Throughout the chapters, we have discovered that Kabbalistic knowledge unfolds in multiple layers, offering not only explanations about the nature of the cosmos but also practical tools for introspection, healing, and inner transformation.

The Tree of Life and the Process of Self-Knowledge

One of the first central concepts we explored was the Tree of Life, with its ten Sefirot. The Tree of Life serves as a map of both the universe and the human psyche. Each Sefirah represents an aspect of creation and, at the same time, a facet of the soul. By understanding the interconnection between these different aspects, we begin to see the universe as a web of energies, where the divine and the human coexist and interact continuously.

This structure is not merely theoretical. For the Kabbalist, the Tree of Life is a tool for self-knowledge. When we meditate on the Sefirot, we learn to identify where our own energies are blocked or imbalanced. For example, we may realize that our Chesed (loving-kindness) is abundant but not balanced by Gevurah (discipline). Or we may discover that our Keter (crown, connection to the divine) is obscured by material concerns, preventing us from reaching a higher level of spiritual understanding.

The beauty of Kabbalah lies in its practicality. The Tree of Life is not an abstract concept but a structure that invites us to apply its balance in our daily lives. Each Sefirah has its expression in the way we interact with the world and with others. When we live consciously within this structure, we align our own existence with the cosmic order, allowing divine energies to flow more freely through us.

Another fundamental concept we explored was that of duality in the Kabbalistic system. Light and darkness, masculine and feminine, good and evil – these polarities are present at all levels of creation. Kabbalah teaches that creation is the result of the tension between these opposing forces. Without darkness, light cannot be recognized; without evil, free will and spiritual growth would have no purpose.

However, duality is not the ultimate goal. The true goal is unity – the integration of opposing forces in harmony. The Kabbalistic journey is, therefore, a journey of integration, where we learn to recognize and balance the tensions in our own lives. Often, we find ourselves struggling with opposing forces within us – material desire versus spiritual desire, selfishness versus altruism. Kabbalah teaches us to embrace these tensions as an essential part of the human experience, but it also guides us on how to transcend them, integrating these forces to achieve inner unity.

Kabbalistic practice involves working with these polarities consciously, balancing our inclinations, and learning to see the interconnectedness of all things. This is a continuous process, as creation and correction are never complete. Spiritual work is a constant cycle of creation, destruction, and renewal, both in our individual lives and in the world as a whole.

Another powerful teaching of Kabbalah is that the human being is not just a passive witness to the cosmic process. On the contrary, we are co-creators, active participants in the manifestation of reality. The concept of Tikun Olam, or the correction of the world, reinforces this idea. The world is not complete; it is in constant evolution, and each of us has a role to play in this process of correction and improvement.

The spiritual practices we have explored throughout this book—meditations, prayers, acts of kindness—are all forms of co-creation. Every action we perform with spiritual intention, every elevated thought, and every conscious choice we make impacts not only our own lives but the universe as a whole. Kabbalah constantly reminds us that we are responsible for our own evolution and for the state of the world around us.

This responsibility may seem overwhelming, but it is also a profound source of power and empowerment. Knowing that our choices have a real impact offers us a unique opportunity to live with purpose. At every moment, we have the chance to choose light over darkness, unity over separation, kindness over selfishness. And each of these choices contributes to Tikun Olam, accelerating the process of global correction.

The study of Kabbalah is not limited to an intellectual accumulation of information. From the first chapters, we emphasized that Kabbalistic knowledge is transformative. As we understand the spiritual laws that govern the universe, we begin to see our own lives in a new light. The challenges we face gain a deeper meaning, and the blessings we receive are seen as part of a continuous flow of divine energy.

Transformation happens when we apply Kabbalistic knowledge in our daily lives. This means that the spiritual journey is not something separate from our everyday experiences but is intimately connected to them. By applying the teachings on the Sefirot, the Divine Names, and meditation, we begin to shape our lives according to spiritual principles. This process of transformation is gradual and continuous, but its effects are profound.

For many, the study of Kabbalah is the beginning of an endless path. With each layer of knowledge we uncover, we find new mysteries and new opportunities for spiritual growth. Kabbalah invites us to become eternal students, always seeking the next revelation, always open to transformation.

It is important to remember that, although the spiritual journey is deeply personal, it never happens in isolation. As we have seen, all souls are connected, and each individual action has repercussions on the collective. Kabbalah teaches us that the destiny of humanity is intertwined, and that the spiritual progress of a single individual can elevate the entire field of global consciousness.

Therefore, spiritual practice also involves a commitment to others. Kabbalah deeply values community, the act of giving, and the recognition that our own evolution is directly linked to the evolution of those around us. Thus, the spiritual journey is not only about our own enlightenment but about how we can contribute to the enlightenment of the world.

As we approach the end of this journey, it is essential to recognize that Kabbalah does not offer a static end. It is a living path, in constant motion, and those who commit to its teachings discover that there is always more to learn, more to experience, and more to transform.

Understanding the Kabbalistic journey is more than an intellectual or theoretical exercise. It is about a continuous spiritual transformation that challenges us to delve into every aspect of our existence and connection with the divine. As we consolidate our learning and integrate the teachings acquired throughout this work, it is important to highlight how this wisdom can continue to shape and illuminate our lives, regardless of the challenges we encounter along the way.

Kabbalah, as we have seen, offers not only an understanding of creation, cosmic forces, and the nature of reality but also a set of practical tools that can be applied daily. These teachings empower us to act as co-creators in the universe and help us balance our internal and external forces, always with the aim of achieving greater unity and harmony, both on a personal and collective level.

To successfully follow the Kabbalistic path, a daily spiritual practice is essential. This does not imply that everyone should follow the same routines, but that each individual develops a system that resonates with their spiritual needs and their level of understanding.

Meditation on the Sefirot: A powerful and transformative practice is meditation on the Sefirot of the Tree of Life. This can be done daily, focusing on one Sefirah at a time. Through visualization, introspection, and contemplation, we can balance the energies associated with each of the divine emanations, aligning our actions with the spiritual flow of the universe. This practice helps to identify areas of imbalance and to bring healing and harmony to our personal and collective lives.

Continuous Study: Kabbalah is a never-ending study. The Zohar, the Sefer Yetzirah, and other Kabbalistic texts contain layers of wisdom that can be discovered over a lifetime. Setting aside time for reading and contemplation of these sacred texts not only increases our knowledge but also connects us directly with the spiritual energy that flows through these teachings.

Gematria and Hidden Meanings: The practice of Gematria, the numerical study of Hebrew letters, can also be a practical tool for illuminating hidden aspects of life. The analysis of words, names, and events in light of Kabbalistic numerology reveals hidden patterns and meanings, allowing us to see beyond the surface and grasp the spiritual depth of reality.

Use of Divine Names: Working with the Divine Names is a central practice in Kabbalah. These names, such as the Tetragrammaton (YHVH), possess specific energies that can be invoked for meditation, healing, and protection. Learning to use them consciously, whether through prayer or meditation, gives us access to deeper levels of connection with the divine and with the powers of creation.

Tikun Olam: The concept of Tikun Olam should not be forgotten in daily practice. By making choices that heal the world, whether through acts of kindness, justice, or spiritual elevation, we contribute directly to the correction of the universe. Small gestures of altruism, honesty, and empathy resonate in the global spiritual field, accelerating the process of redemption and transformation.

After absorbing the fundamentals of Kabbalah, many wonder, "What comes next?" The next step is to develop a spiritual independence that allows the practitioner to navigate the teachings and practices of Kabbalah autonomously. This means building a solid and adaptable spiritual routine, adjusting as the needs of the soul and the circumstances of life change.

For this, continuity in some fundamental pillars is recommended:

Regular Study: Never stop studying. Kabbalistic practice is based on the constant pursuit of knowledge. New interpretations and levels of understanding are always within reach of those who dedicate themselves to constant study. In addition, the act of studying itself elevates the soul and connects us with divine wisdom.

Spiritual Community: Although the spiritual journey is individual, Kabbalah greatly values interaction within a community. Exchanging ideas, sharing experiences, and studying in a group can bring new insights and strengthen everyone's spiritual path. Connection with others who also follow the Kabbalistic path is a powerful form of support and growth.

Self-Correction and Continuous Reflection: The practice of regular introspection is vital for spiritual progress. Setting aside moments to evaluate thoughts, actions, and intentions keeps us on the path of personal rectification. Self-correction is a constant process in the Kabbalistic journey, where we learn to recognize our faults, accept responsibility for them, and seek to improve constantly.

Connection with the Divine: Meditation and prayer are the main forms of connection with higher energies. Setting aside time daily to connect with the divine is essential to keep alive the spiritual flame that guides the Kabbalistic path. Each prayer, each moment of contemplation, serves as a reminder that we are in a divine partnership, co-creating reality at every instant.

In addition to the practices mentioned, expanding knowledge of Kabbalah through other sources and teachers is also recommended. Books, classes, and seminars conducted by Kabbalah scholars can offer new horizons and deepen the understanding of what has already been learned. The study of Kabbalah is not fixed or static; it evolves with the practitioner and continuously offers new levels of understanding.

The exploration of new themes within Kabbalah, such as Kabbalistic astrology, the relationship with spiritual healing, and the deepening of meditative practices with the 72 Names of God, can open new doors for the expansion of the soul. The Kabbalistic universe is vast and multifaceted, and each individual will find their own path of exploration and expansion within this sacred system.

Kabbalah teaches us that time is not linear but cyclical. Jewish holidays, the rhythms of nature, and the cycles of the soul are all interconnected, and recognizing these cycles in our own lives is fundamental to living in accordance with the divine flow. Each phase of our life—whether of growth, stagnation, or renewal—has its role within the spiritual context. Learning to align ourselves with these cycles allows us to flow more harmoniously with the universe.

Kabbalah suggests that we tune in to the energies of cosmic cycles, especially through the observance and celebration of Jewish holidays, which are spiritual portals for personal renewal and correction. Understanding the energies of each season and holiday, and how they apply to our own spiritual journey, can be a continuous source of guidance and inspiration.

As we consolidate all the learning acquired in this work, it is essential to remember that Kabbalah is not a final destination, but a continuous process of seeking, discovery, and correction. Each teaching we have explored throughout this book – from the Sefirot to Gematria, from the Divine Names to the integration of the ego – should be applied as a compass that guides our spiritual life.

However, each individual is responsible for continuing the journey on their own. Kabbalah does not impose fixed or absolute dogmas; instead, it offers tools for each soul to seek its own connection with the divine, in a unique and personal way.

This book was only the beginning of a spiritual journey that can last a lifetime, or more. Each step on the Kabbalistic path brings us closer to self-knowledge, unity with the divine, and active contribution to the correction of the world. As the reader advances, new challenges will arise, but also new revelations and moments of profound spiritual connection.

May this be just the first of many steps on your Kabbalistic journey. The knowledge and practices shared here are seeds that, when cultivated with dedication and love, will blossom into wisdom, transformation, and light. May your journey be filled with discovery, growth, and continuous spiritual elevation.

Epilogue

At the end of this journey, you are no longer the same. The secrets revealed by Kabbalah echo in your mind and in your heart, and now, what remains is a choice: how will you integrate this knowledge into your daily life? Every concept, every vision explored throughout these pages, was an invitation to transformation. Tikun Olam—the repair of the world—begins with your own transformation. The understanding of the spiritual worlds, the Sephirot, the divine names, and the forces that move the universe is now a part of you.

Kabbalah teaches us that nothing is static. Creation is a constant flow, and you, as a human being, are a co-creator in this process. With every action, you contribute to balance or to chaos, to light or to darkness. But there is no irreconcilable duality. Good and evil, light and shadow, are all part of the same whole. True wisdom lies in understanding how these forces intertwine and, from that understanding, acting to restore harmony.

Now, what will you do with this knowledge? Kabbalistic practice is not something that ends with the last page of this book. It is a path that unfolds infinitely before you. The world around you is the stage where you can apply everything you have learned. Every decision you make, every word you say, will be an opportunity to align yourself with the divine forces, to manifest what is just, beautiful, and true.

Kabbalah has taught you that each of us carries a divine spark, and that this spark always seeks to return to its source. Your life, with all its joys and challenges, is the field where this spark can shine, where you can contribute to the great work of repairing the world. There is no act too small. A simple gesture of kindness, a word of compassion, a conscious reflection can be what is needed for the forces of the universe to realign more harmoniously.

But remember: this path is continuous. What you have learned here is only the beginning. The wisdom of Kabbalah is a vast ocean, and you have only just begun to navigate its waters. Keep exploring, keep delving deeper, because the layers of knowledge are infinite. Each new discovery will be a new door to dimensions of understanding that, for now, are unimaginable.

This is not the end of the journey, but the beginning of a life of awareness. Kabbalah is now a part of you, a living tool that will guide you in every step from here on. As you look to the future, see it as an opportunity to continue growing, to continue transforming, to continue seeking the lost unity, not only in yourself but in everything around you.

You are ready to live with more presence, more meaning, and more purpose. The world needs your light. May you continue to walk this path of wisdom and, with each step, contribute to a more harmonious and enlightened universe. The journey continues.

www.ingramcontent.com/pod-product-compliance
Lightning Source LLC
LaVergne TN
LVHW040136080526
838202LV00042B/2923